MANZIL

Duas from the Noble
Quran, For Protection and
Success.

Dr. Abdullah Aslam

CONTENTS

PREFACE

بِسْمِ ٱللَّهِ ٱلرَّحْمَٰنِ ٱلرَّحِيمِ

In the name of Allah, the Most Beneficent, Most Merciful...
All praises to Allah Almighty, peace and blessings of Allah be

upon His Messenger, Prophet Muhammad (ﷺ), his family

members and his companions.

I extend my gratitude to Allah (ﷻ), for the ability to share

the knowledge and understandings from the research of the daily
Islamic practices of Maulana Muḥammad Zakarīyā ibn
Muḥammad Yaḥyá Ṣiddīqī Kāndhlawī Sahāranpūrī Muhājir
Madanī—popularly known as a "Hazrat Shaykh al-Hadith"—who
was a known figure in the study of Hadiths.

This book will be focusing on some of the issues related to the
daily practice of Manzil in terms of introduction, reciting
method, Benefits and the Quranic Verses in Manzil citing relating
Hadiths and their translations. It also contains translations and
transliterations of the verses along with detailed explanations.

Most of the translations of the Quranic verses featured in this
book are quoted from The Interpretations of Yusuf 'Ali (1999),
published by Amana Publication, USA. All the hadiths cited in the

4

book were considered to follow the method set forth by Imam al-Nawawi. Most of the Hadiths are quoted from Sahih al-Bukhari, Sahih Muslim, Sunan Ibn Majah, Jami` at-Tirmidhi, Sunan an-Nasa'i, Sunan Abi Dawud.

I hope that this book will be utilized by Muslims for strengthening their *ibadah*; so that they are always in the grace and protection of Allah (ﷻ).

INTRODUCTION

Manzil Dua is a collection of Ayaat and short Surahs from the Quran that are to be recited as a means of protection, an antidote - *Ruqya (i.e., recite supplication or Quranic Ayat and blow)* against Black Magic, Jinn, Witchcraft, Sihr, Sorcery, Evil Eye and the like as well as other harmful evil forces.

If you thought, Black Magic, Witchcraft, Sihr, Sorcery, Evil Eye... are all rubbish—you were wrong. The concept of sorcery or witchcraft exists in Islam. In the Qur'an, verse 102 of Chapter Al-Baqara states:

وَٱتَّبَعُواْ مَا تَتْلُواْ ٱلشَّيَاطِينُ عَلَىٰ مُلْكِ سُلَيْمَٰنَ ۖ وَمَا كَفَرَ سُلَيْمَٰنُ وَلَٰكِنَّ ٱلشَّيَاطِينَ كَفَرُواْ يُعَلِّمُونَ ٱلنَّاسَ ٱلسِّحْرَ وَمَا أُنزِلَ عَلَى ٱلْمَلَكَيْنِ بِبَابِلَ هَٰرُوتَ وَمَٰرُوتَ ۚ وَمَا يُعَلِّمَانِ مِنْ أَحَدٍ حَتَّىٰ يَقُولَا إِنَّمَا نَحْنُ فِتْنَةٌ فَلَا تَكْفُرْ ۖ فَيَتَعَلَّمُونَ مِنْهُمَا مَا يُفَرِّقُونَ بِهِۦ بَيْنَ ٱلْمَرْءِ وَزَوْجِهِۦ ۚ وَمَا هُم بِضَآرِّينَ بِهِۦ مِنْ أَحَدٍ إِلَّا بِإِذْنِ ٱللَّهِ ۚ وَيَتَعَلَّمُونَ مَا يَضُرُّهُمْ وَلَا يَنفَعُهُمْ ۚ وَلَقَدْ عَلِمُواْ لَمَنِ ٱشْتَرَىٰهُ مَا لَهُۥ فِى ٱلْءَاخِرَةِ مِنْ خَلَٰقٍ ۚ وَلَبِئْسَ مَا شَرَوْاْ بِهِۦٓ أَنفُسَهُمْ ۚ لَوْ كَانُواْ يَعْلَمُونَ ﴿١٠٢﴾

And they followed [instead] what the devils had recited during the reign of Solomon. It was not Solomon who disbelieved, but the devils disbelieved, teaching people magic and that which was revealed to the two angels at Babylon, Harut and Marut. But the two angels do not teach anyone unless they say, "We are a trial, so do not disbelieve [by practising magic]." And [yet] they learn from them that by which they cause separation between a man and his wife. But they do not harm anyone through it except by permission of Allah. And the people learn what harms them and does not benefit them. But the Children of Israel certainly knew that whoever purchased the magic would not have in the Hereafter any share. And wretched is that for which they sold themselves if they only knew. (102)

The Qur'an and the Sunnah of Muhammad (ﷺ) have been sent down to us—Muslims—as guides, on how to live our lives completely; as believers in Allah (ﷻ). These two books contain so many powerful verses and supplications that give us protection from evil, from debt and even verses and duas that protect us and our families. As the Holy Prophet (ﷺ) taught his companions and the people who came after them, every dua or verse of protection has been given to us by Allah (ﷻ), and we should use them to not only protect ourselves in this life but also as protection for the hereafter.

There are so many verses of the Holy Qur'an that serve a purpose for us beyond reading them and earning rewards. Some of which are these verses that we have mentioned as verses that we use to protect ourselves and our families from harm. And even though there are many more that you will discover as you understand the Qur'an more, these are good for us to start protecting ourselves with every day.

In the tradition of Prophet Muhammad (ﷺ), he was himself once targeted by sorcerers, but he annulled their effect through the recitation of certain verses of the Quran. As indicated by different traditions, distinctive parts of the Qur'an are depicted to positively affect a person in terms of negating and eliminating the effects of witchcraft, or for general prosperity and improvement as a honing Muslim. There are several benefits of reading manzil dua, as you will be free from any evil spell cast on you. You will be safe from all the evil forces which dwell and none of them can harm you or your loved ones. The manzil dua may be used for many other purposes as well.

It was narrated that Abu Hurairah said:

"The Prophet (ﷺ) came to visit me (when I was sick), and said to me: 'Shall I not recite for you a Ruqyah (i.e., recite supplication or Quranic Ayat and blow) that Jibra'il brought to me?' I said: 'May my father and mother be ransomed for you! Yes, O Messenger of Allah!' He said: Bismillah arqika, wallahu yashfika, min kulli da'in fika, min sharrin- naffathati fil-'uqad, wa min sharri hasidin idha hasad (In the Name of Allah I perform Ruqyah for you, from every disease that is in you, and from the evil of those who (practice witchcraft when they) blow in the knots, and from the evil of the envier when he envies), three times."

حَدَّثَنَا مُحَمَّدُ بْنُ بَشَّارٍ وَحَفْصُ بْنُ عُمَرَ قَالاَ حَدَّثَنَا عَبْدُ الرَّحْمَنِ حَدَّثَنَا سُفْيَانُ عَنْ عَاصِمِ بْنِ عُبَيْدِ اللَّهِ عَنْ زِيَادِ بْنِ ثُوَيْبٍ عَنْ أَبِي هُرَيْرَةَ قَالَ جَاءَ النَّبِيُّ ـ صلى الله عليه وسلم ـ يَعُودُنِي فَقَالَ لِي " أَلاَ أَرْقِيكَ بِرُقْيَةٍ جَاءَنِي بِهَا جِبْرَائِيلُ " . قُلْتُ بِأَبِي وَأُمِّي بَلَى يَا رَسُولَ اللَّهِ . قَالَ " بِسْمِ اللَّهِ أَرْقِيكَ وَاللَّهُ يَشْفِيكَ مِنْ كُلِّ دَاءٍ فِيكَ مِنْ شَرِّ النَّفَّاثَاتِ فِي الْعُقَدِ وَمِنْ شَرِّ حَاسِدٍ إِذَا حَسَدَ " . ثَلاَثَ مَرَّاتٍ .

Grade: Da'if (Darussalam)

Reference: Sunan Ibn Majah 3524
In-book Reference: Book 31, Hadith 89
English **Translation:** Vol. 4, Book 31, Hadith 3524

Abu Sa'eed narrated that:

Jibril came to the Prophet (ﷺ) and said: "O Muhammad! Are you suffering?" He said: "Yes." He said: "In the Name of Allah, I recite a prayer (Ruqyah) over you, from the evil of every person and the evil eye. In the Name of Allah, I recite a prayer (Ruqyah) over you, may Allah cure you."

حَدَّثَنَا بِشْرُ بْنُ هِلاَلٍ الْبَصْرِيُّ الصَّوَّافُ، حَدَّثَنَا عَبْدُ الْوَارِثِ بْنُ سَعِيدٍ، عَنْ عَبْدِ الْعَزِيزِ بْنِ صُهَيْبٍ، عَنْ أَبِي نَضْرَةَ، عَنْ أَبِي سَعِيدٍ، أَنَّ جِبْرِيلَ، أَتَى النَّبِيَّ صلى الله عليه وسلم فَقَالَ يَا مُحَمَّدُ اشْتَكَيْتَ قَالَ " نَعَمْ " . قَالَ بِاسْمِ اللَّهِ أَرْقِيكَ مِنْ كُلِّ شَيْءٍ يُؤْذِيكَ مِنْ شَرِّ كُلِّ نَفْسٍ

9

وَعَيْنِ حَاسِدٍ بِاسْمِ اللَّهِ أَرْقِيكَ وَاللَّهُ يَشْفِيكَ .

Grade: Sahih (Darussalam)

Reference: Jami` at-Tirmidhi 972
In-book Reference: Book 10, Hadith 8
English **Translation:** Vol. 2, Book 5, Hadith 972

In This book, we will discuss a little about how to practice the verses in Manzil, the order to recite them based on Hadiths, and the verses with their translation.

MANZIL RECITATION METHOD

Manzil Dua is to be recited twice a day, in the morning and the evening. As Allah (ﷻ) encourages glorifying and remembering Him in the morning and evening, as stated in the Quran:

$$﴾ ٤٢ ﴿ وَسَبِّحُوهُ بُكْرَةً وَأَصِيلًا$$

Translation: And exalt Him morning and evening. (Surah al-Ahzab, 33: 42)

When the Messenger (ﷺ) of Allah is being showered with taunts and abuses by the enemies and his companions were made the target of a propaganda campaign to frustrate his mission, the messenger said: the believers should neither listen to these absurd things unconcerned, nor should become themselves also involved in the doubts and suspicions spread by the enemies, nor should resort to abusive language in retaliation, but they should turn to Allah (ﷻ) and remember Him more than usual as a special measure. "Glorify Him morning and evening" means to glorify Allah (ﷻ) constantly, to express His holiness and purity by word of mouth and not merely by counting beads on the rosary.

In another verse, Allah (ﷻ) also commands:

$$\text{وَٱذۡكُرِ ٱسۡمَ رَبِّكَ بُكۡرَةً وَأَصِيلًا ﴿٢٥﴾ وَمِنَ ٱلَّيۡلِ فَٱسۡجُدۡ لَهُ}$$

$$\text{وَسَبِّحۡهُ لَيۡلًا طَوِيلًا ﴿٢٦﴾}$$

Translation: And celebrate the name of thy Lord morning and evening. And prostrate yourself before Him at night, and extol His Glory during the long watches of the night. (Surah al-Insan, 76: 25-26)

To remember Allah (ﷻ) morning and evening may also imply remembering Allah (ﷻ) always but when the command to remember Allah (ﷻ) at specific times is given, it implies the Salat (Prayer). In this verse, bukrah means the morning and asil the time from the sun's decline till sunset, which covers the Zuhr and the Asr times. The night starts after sunset; therefore, the command "to prostrate yourself in the night" would apply to both the Maghrib and the Isha Prayers. Then, the command "to glorify Allah(ﷻ) in the long hours of the night", clearly points to the time of the Tahajjud Prayer. This also shows that these have been the Prayer times in Islam from the beginning. However, the command making the Prayer obligatory five times a day with fixed times and several rakahs was given on the occasion of Mi'raj (ascension).

12

قَالَ الْإِمَامُ جَعْفَرُ بْنُ مُحَمَّدٍ الصَّادِقُ)عَلَيْهِ السَّلَامُ :(أَلْقُرْآنُ عَهْدُ اللهِ إِلَى خَلْقِهِ فَقَدْ يَنْبَغِي لِلْمَرْءِ الْمُسْلِمِ أَنْ يَنْظُرَ فِي عَهْدِهِ وَ إِنْ يَقْرَأُ مِنَ الْقُرْآنِ فِي كُلِّ يَوْمٍ خَمْسِينَ آيَةٍ.

Imam Ja'far ibn Muhammad as-Sadiq (peace be upon him) has said: "The Qur'an is the trust of Allah (given) to His creations; therefore, it is desirable for every Muslim to look at this trust and to recite (a minimum of) 50 ayat (verses) of the Qur'an every day."

Usulul Kafi, Volume 2, Page 609

قَالَ رَسُولُ اللهِ)صَلَّى اللهُ عَلَيْهِ وَ آلِهِ وَ سَلَّمَ :(مَنْ قَرَأَ عَشْرَ آيَاتٍ فِي لَيْلَةٍ لَمْ يُكْتَبْ مِنَ الْغَافِلِينَ وَ مَنْ قَرَأَ خَمْسِينَ آيَةٍ كُتِبَ مِنَ الذَّاكِرِينَ وَ مَنْ قَرَأَ مِائَةَ آيَةٍ كُتِبَ مِنَ الْقَانِتِينَ.

The Messenger of Allah (blessings of Allah (ﷺ) be upon him and his family) has said: "One who recites ten verses (ayat) of the Qur'an every night will not be counted amongst the negligent ones (Ghafilin), and one who recites fifty verses (ayat) will be written as those who remember Allah (Dhakirin), and one who recites one hundred verses (ayat) will be written down as the obedient and worshipper of Allah (Qanitin)."

Thawabul A'mal, Page 232

قَالَ أَمِيرُ الْمُؤْمِنِينَ عَلِيُّ ابْنُ أَبِي طَالِبٍ (عَلَيْهِ السَّلَامُ): (مَنْ قَرَأَ مِائَةَ آيَةٍ مِنَ الْقُرْآنِ مِنْ أَيِّ الْقُرْآنَ شَاءَ ثُمَّ قَالَ سَبْعَ مَرَّاتٍ)): يَا أَللَّهُ ((فَلَوْ دَعَا عَلَى الصَّخْرَةِ لَقَلَعَهَا إِنْشَاءَ اللَّهُ.

Amirul Mo'minin 'Ali ibn Abi Talib (peace be upon him) has said: "A person who recites 100 verses from anywhere in the Qur'an and then says: 'Ya Allah' seven times if he wanted to remove a huge boulder (from the ground), he would be able to do so with the permission of Allah."

Thawabul A'mal, Page 233

Narrated Abdullah ibn Amr ibn al-'As:

The Prophet (ﷺ) said: If anyone prays at night reciting

regularly ten verses, he will not be recorded among the negligent; if anyone prays at night and recites a hundred verses,

he will be recorded among those who are obedient to Allah (ﷻ);

and if anyone prays at night reciting one thousand verses, he will be recorded among those who receive huge rewards.

Abu Dawud said: The name of Ibn Hujairah al-Asghar is 'Abd Allah b. 'Abd al-Rahman b. Hujairah.

حَدَّثَنَا أَحْمَدُ بْنُ صَالِحٍ، حَدَّثَنَا ابْنُ وَهْبٍ، أَخْبَرَنَا عَمْرُو، أَنَّ أَبَا سَوِيَّةَ، حَدَّثَهُ أَنَّهُ، سَمِعَ ابْنَ حُجَيْرَةَ، يُخْبِرُ عَنْ عَبْدِ اللَّهِ بْنِ عَمْرِو بْنِ الْعَاصِ، قَالَ قَالَ رَسُولُ اللَّهِ صلى الله عليه وسلم " مَنْ قَامَ بِعَشْرِ آيَاتٍ لَمْ يُكْتَبْ مِنَ الْغَافِلِينَ وَمَنْ قَامَ بِمِائَةِ آيَةٍ كُتِبَ مِنَ الْقَانِتِينَ وَمَنْ قَامَ

14

بِأَلْفِ آيَةٍ كُتِبَ مِنَ الْمُقَنْطِرِينَ " . قَالَ أَبُو دَاوُدَ ابْنُ حُجَيْرَةَ الْأَصْغَرُ عَبْدُ اللَّهِ بْنُ عَبْدِ الرَّحْمَنِ بْنِ حُجَيْرَةَ .

Grade: Sahih (Al-Albani)

Reference: Sunan Abi Dawud 1398
In-book Reference: Book 6, Hadith 28
English **Translation:** Book 6, Hadith 1393

If one chooses to practice it once a day, it is advisable to recite it at night especially after Maghrib and before going to bed, preferably at the same hour and time every day according to the suitability of one's time. To reinforce this statement, the following hadith demands a Muslim to read 100 verses at night:

Imaam Ahmad narrates from Tameem ad-Daaree (RA) who said the Messenger of Allaah (ﷺ) said, "Whoever recited 100 verses in the night then it is written form him as if he recited the whole night." (Musnad Ahmad 28/156 no.16958) al-Arnaa'oot and his associates authenticated it.

Abu Darda' narrated: Prophet Muhammad (ﷺ) said, "Whoever recites 100 verses at night, he will not be recorded as one of the heedless." (Al-Darimi, 2000: 3491)

In light of the encouragement to recite at least 100 Quranic verses, most scholars have suggested reciting the Manzil. This has been practised by many eminent scholars and is known to have been compiled by Shaykh Zakariyya of Saharanpur Daruloom many decades ago.

MANZIL DUA BENEFITS

Manzil is recited for protection and as an antidote for illness. This dua is so powerful for removing every kind of sickness, *Alhamdulillah*. Once you do it with all your devotion Insha Allah

(﷾) you will get positive results. There are a lot of benefits of

Manzil Dua (collection of Quranic verses). Let us discuss the prominent benefits or advantages below:

Manzil Dua for Protection Against Calamities

The main purpose of reciting manzil dua is for protection. In

this mortal world, what we pray the most—from Allah (﷾)—is

for our and our family's protection; from every negative aspect of this and the afterlife. Unless we are protected, we are never totally safe and anything can happen at any time, which can threaten our health and *Imaan*. There are many ways the devil or *shaitan* could ism guide you and play with your urges and desires. You may also be under the influence of the jinns. There are so many dangers around us that we cannot simply escape, the prying *shaitan* or an evil jinn and other evil forces; it is impossible to make yourself safe from these forces by yourself, as they may attack you at any moment. You will not even realise when you are being possessed, but you will experience and cause great harm not only to yourself but also for the others, dearer you. To protect yourself and your family from all kinds of evil forces that you may face in your life, you should start reciting the manzil dua for protection. This dua is a very effective method to ensure that all evil forces keep away from you and that you stay protected.

Manzil Dua for Protection Against Evil Eye

The word evil eye comes from the Arabic word "al-ayn." It refers to a scenario when a person harms another with his eyes. The evil eye represents an arrow coming from the depth of a soul of a person, who is jealous of you or of what you have in your possession and considers you as his enemy. An evil eye can harm anyone even unintentionally. However, there are grievous effects of the evil eye also; you may start to experience bad events in life continuously. These can be cured through these Quranic Verses known as Manzil Dua. In certain cases, one can recite manzil dua (the entire collection of Quranic verses) in an ablution. This will ward off the evil effects from the patient if

ALLAH (ﷻ) The Exalted wills.

There are many among our Muslim brethren, who think that the evil eye is not real. They should read this hadith, reported by Ibn Abbas (May Allah be pleased with him),

Ibn 'Abbas (May Allah be pleased with him) reported Allah's Messenger (ﷺ) as saying:

The influence of an evil eye is a fact; if anything would precede destiny it would be the influence of an evil eye.

،وَحَدَّثَنَا عَبْدُ اللَّهِ بْنُ عَبْدِ الرَّحْمَنِ الدَّارِمِيُّ، وَحَجَّاجُ بْنُ الشَّاعِرِ وَأَحْمَدُ بْنُ خِرَاشٍ، قَالَ عَبْدُ اللَّهِ أَخْبَرَنَا وَقَالَ الآخَرَانِ، حَدَّثَنَا مُسْلِمُ بْنُ إِبْرَاهِيمَ، قَالَ حَدَّثَنَا وُهَيْبٌ، عَنِ ابْنِ، طَاوُسٍ عَنْ أَبِيهِ، عَنِ ابْنِ عَبَّاسٍ، عَنِ النَّبِيِّ صلى الله عليه وسلم قَالَ "الْعَيْنُ حَقٌّ وَلَوْ كَانَ شَىْءٌ سَابَقَ الْقَدَرَ سَبَقَتْهُ الْعَيْنُ وَإِذَا اسْتُغْسِلْتُمْ فَاغْسِلُوا".

Reference: Sahih Muslim 2188
In-book Reference: Book 39, Hadith 56
USC-MSA web (English) Reference: Book 26, Hadith 5427

Manzil Dua for Success

Manzil dua can also be recited to resolve any sort of issues or obstacles in way of your success. These issues could be family problems, financial crisis, frequent rejection of marriage proposals or any other worldly obstacles. Recite Manzil Dua every day and make a prayer for the resolution of your respective issue(s). This will also surely forcefully nullify any evil effects like black magic or sorcery if done in the marriage. However, every hard try needs to be implemented with dedication and devotion. This Quranic verse should be recited with all-around concentration. One of the most significant points to be taken care of is the correct pronunciation of the Quranic words. The reciter should read the verses accurately and calmly.

HADITH REGARDING QURAN VERSES (MANZIL/*Ruqyah*) FOR CURE

The recital of Quran verses during illness, and other maladies and for protection, has been practised by the Prophet (ﷺ) and many Muslims for centuries. The following Hadiths suggest the same:

◆ **Narrated ʿAisha (May Allah be pleased with her):**

Whenever Allah's Messenger (ﷺ) became sick, he would recite **Mu'awwidhat** (*Surat Al-Falaq and Surat An- Nas*) and then blow his breath over his body. When he became seriously ill, I used to recite (these two Suras) and rub his hands over his body hoping for its blessings.

حَدَّثَنَا عَبْدُ اللهِ بْنُ يُوسُفَ، أَخْبَرَنَا مَالِكٌ، عَنِ ابْنِ شِهَابٍ، عَنْ

عُرْوَةَ، عَنْ عَائِشَةَ، رضى الله عنها أَنَّ رَسُولَ اللهِ صلى الله عليه وسلم

كَانَ إِذَا اشْتَكَى يَقْرَأُ عَلَى نَفْسِهِ بِالْمُعَوِّذَاتِ وَيَنْفُثُ، فَلَمَّا اشْتَدَّ وَجَعُهُ

كُنْتُ أَقْرَأُ عَلَيْهِ وَأَمْسَحُ بِيَدِهِ رَجَاءَ بَرَكَتِهَا.

Reference: Sahih al-Bukhari 5016
In-book Reference: Book 66, Hadith 38
USC-MSA web (English) Reference: Vol. 6, Book 61, Hadith 535

◆ **Narrated `Aisha (May Allah be pleased with her):**

Whenever Allah's Messenger (ﷺ) went to bed, he used to

recite Surat-al-Ikhlas, Surat-al-Falaq and Surat-an- Nas and then blow on his palms and pass them over his face and those parts of his body that his hands could reach. And when he fell ill, he used to order me to do like that for him.

حَدَّثَنَا عَبْدُ الْعَزِيزِ بْنُ عَبْدِ اللَّهِ الأُوَيْسِيُّ، حَدَّثَنَا سُلَيْمَانُ، عَنْ يُونُسَ، عَنِ ابْنِ شِهَابٍ، عَنْ عُرْوَةَ بْنِ الزُّبَيْرِ، عَنْ عَائِشَةَ ـ رضى الله عنها ـ قَالَتْ كَانَ رَسُولُ اللَّهِ صلى الله عليه وسلم إِذَا أَوَى إِلَى فِرَاشِهِ نَفَثَ فِي كَفَّيْهِ بِقُلْ هُوَ اللَّهُ أَحَدٌ وَبِالْمُعَوِّذَتَيْنِ جَمِيعًا، ثُمَّ يَمْسَحُ بِهِمَا وَجْهَهُ، وَمَا بَلَغَتْ يَدَاهُ مِنْ جَسَدِهِ. قَالَتْ عَائِشَةُ فَلَمَّا اشْتَكَى كَانَ يَأْمُرُنِي أَنْ أَفْعَلَ ذَلِكَ بِهِ. قَالَ يُونُسُ كُنْتُ أَرَى ابْنَ شِهَابٍ يَصْنَعُ ذَلِكَ إِذَا أَتَى إِلَى فِرَاشِهِ.

Reference: Sahih al-Bukhari 5748
In-book Reference: Book 76, Hadith 63
USC-MSA web (English) Reference: Vol. 7, Book 71, Hadith 644

◆ **It was narrated from 'Aishah (May Allah be pleased with her):**

the Prophet (ﷺ) commanded her to recite **Ruqyah** (i.e.,

recite supplication or Quranic Ayat and blow) to treat the evil eye.

حَدَّثَنَا عَلِيُّ بْنُ أَبِي الْخَصِيبِ، حَدَّثَنَا وَكِيعٌ، عَنْ سُفْيَانَ، وَمِسْعَرٍ عَنْ مَعْبَدِ بْنِ خَالِدٍ، عَنْ عَبْدِ اللَّهِ بْنِ شَدَّادٍ، عَنْ عَائِشَةَ، أَنَّ النَّبِيَّ ـ صلى الله عليه وسلم ـ أَمَرَهَا أَنْ تَسْتَرْقِيَ مِنَ الْعَيْنِ

Grade: Sahih (Darussalam)

Reference: Sunan Ibn Majah 3512
In-book Reference: Book 31, Hadith 77
English **Translation:** Vol. 4, Book 31, Hadith 3512

◆ **Narrated Ibn `Abbas (May Allah be pleased with him):**

Some of the companions of the Prophet (ﷺ) passed by some

people staying at a place where there was water, and one of those people had been stung by a scorpion. A man from those staying near the water came and said to the companions of the Prophet, "Is there anyone among you who can do Ruqya as near the water there is a person who has been stung by a scorpion." So, one of the Prophet's companions went to him and recited Surat-al-Fatiha for a sheep as his fee. The patient got cured and the man brought the sheep to his companions who disliked that

and said, "You have taken wages for reciting Allah's Book."
When they arrived at Medina, they said, ' O Allah's Messenger
(ﷺ)! (This person) has taken wages for reciting Allah's Book"

On that Allah's Messenger (ﷺ) said, "You are most entitled to

take wages for doing a Ruqya with Allah's Book."

حَدَّثَنِي سِيدَانُ بْنُ مُضَارِبٍ أَبُو مُحَمَّدٍ الْبَاهِلِيُّ، حَدَّثَنَا أَبُو مَعْشَرٍ
الْبَصْرِيُّ ـ هُوَ صَدُوقٌ ـ يُوسُفُ بْنُ يَزِيدَ الْبَرَّاءُ قَالَ حَدَّثَنِي عُبَيْدُ اللَّهِ
بْنُ الأَخْنَسِ أَبُو مَالِكٍ، عَنِ ابْنِ أَبِي مُلَيْكَةَ، عَنِ ابْنِ عَبَّاسٍ، أَنَّ نَفَرًا
مِنْ أَصْحَابِ النَّبِيِّ صلى الله عليه وسلم مَرُّوا بِمَاءٍ فِيهِمْ لَدِيغٌ ـ أَوْ
سَلِيمٌ ـ فَعَرَضَ لَهُمْ رَجُلٌ مِنْ أَهْلِ الْمَاءِ فَقَالَ هَلْ فِيكُمْ مِنْ رَاقٍ إِنَّ
فِي الْمَاءِ رَجُلاً لَدِيغًا أَوْ سَلِيمًا. فَانْطَلَقَ رَجُلٌ مِنْهُمْ فَقَرَأَ بِفَاتِحَةِ الْكِتَابِ
عَلَى شَاءٍ، فَبَرَأَ، فَجَاءَ بِالشَّاءِ إِلَى أَصْحَابِهِ فَكَرِهُوا ذَلِكَ وَقَالُوا أَخَذْتَ
عَلَى كِتَابِ اللَّهِ أَجْرًا. حَتَّى قَدِمُوا الْمَدِينَةَ فَقَالُوا يَا رَسُولَ اللَّهِ أَخَذَ عَلَى
كِتَابِ اللَّهِ أَجْرًا. فَقَالَ رَسُولُ اللَّهِ صلى الله عليه وسلم "إِنَّ أَحَقَّ مَا
أَخَذْتُمْ عَلَيْهِ أَجْرًا كِتَابُ اللَّهِ".

Reference: Sahih al-Bukhari 5737
In-book Reference: Book 76, Hadith 52
USC-MSA web (English) Reference: Vol. 7, Book 71, Hadith 633

◆ **Abu Sa'id Al-Khudri (May Allah be pleased with him) reported:**

The Messenger of Allah (ﷺ) used to seek protection against

the evil of jinn and the evil eyes till Surat Al-Falaq and Surat An-Nas were revealed. After they were revealed, he took to them for seeking Allah's protection and left everything beside them.

وعن أبي سعيد الخدري رضي الله عنه قال : كان رسول الله صلى

الله عليه وسلم يتعوذ من الجان، وعين الإنسان، حتى نزلت المعوذتان،

فلما نزلتا، أخذ بهما وترك ما سواهما .

At-Tirmidhi
Reference: Riyad as-Salihin 1015
In-book Reference: Book 8, Hadith 25

◆ **'Abdullah bin Khubaib (May Allah be pleased with him) reported:**

The Messenger of Allah (ﷺ) said to me, "Recite Surat Al-

Ikhlas and Al- Mu'awwidhatain (Surat Al-Falaq and Surat An-Nas) three times at dawn and dusk. It will suffice you in all respects."

وعن عبد الله بن خُبيب -بضم الخاء المعجمة- رضي الله عنه قال:

،قال لي رسول الله صلى الله عليه وسلم: "اقرأ: قل هو الله أحد

والمعوذتين حين تمسي وحين تصبح، ثلاث مرات، تكفيك من كل

شيء". رواه أبو داود والترمذي وقال حديث حسن صحيح .

[Abu Dawud and At-Tirmidhi].
Reference: Riyad as-Salihin 1456
In-book Reference: Book 15, Hadith 49

◆ **Aishah (May Allah be pleased with her) narrated that:**

Every night, when the Prophet (ﷺ) would go to his bed, he

would join his hands, then blow in them, as he recited in them: "Say: He is Allah, the One." And "Say: I seek refuge in the Lord of Al-Falaq" and "Say: I seek refuge in the Lord of mankind." Then he would wipe as much as he was able to of his body with them, beginning with the first of his head and face, and the front of his body. He would do this three times.

حَدَّثَنَا قُتَيْبَةُ، حَدَّثَنَا الْمُفَضَّلُ بْنُ فَضَالَةَ، عَنْ عُقَيْلٍ، عَنِ ابْنِ شِهَابٍ، عَنْ عُرْوَةَ، عَنْ عَائِشَةَ، أَنَّ النَّبِيَّ صلى الله عليه وسلم كَانَ إِذَا أَوَى إِلَى فِرَاشِهِ كُلَّ لَيْلَةٍ جَمَعَ كَفَّيْهِ ثُمَّ نَفَثَ فِيهِمَا فَقَرَأَ فِيهِمَا :) قُلْ هُوَ اللَّهُ أَحَدٌ (وَ :) قُلْ أَعُوذُ بِرَبِّ الْفَلَقِ (وَ :) قُلْ أَعُوذُ بِرَبِّ النَّاسِ (ثُمَّ يَمْسَحُ بِهِمَا مَا اسْتَطَاعَ مِنْ جَسَدِهِ يَبْدَأُ بِهِمَا عَلَى رَأْسِهِ وَوَجْهِهِ وَمَا أَقْبَلَ مِنْ جَسَدِهِ يَفْعَلُ ذَلِكَ ثَلاَثَ مَرَّاتٍ . قَالَ هَذَا حَدِيثٌ حَسَنٌ غَرِيبٌ صَحِيحٌ .

Grade: Sahih (Darussalam)

Reference: Jami` at-Tirmidhi 3402
In-book Reference: Book 48, Hadith 33
English **Translation**: Vol. 6, Book 45, Hadith 3402

◆ **It was narrated that Abu Sa'eed said:**

"The Messenger of Allah (ﷺ) used to seek refuge from the evil eye of the jinn and mankind. When the Mu'awwidhatain* was revealed, he started to recite them and stopped reciting anything else."

حَدَّثَنَا أَبُو بَكْرِ بْنُ أَبِي شَيْبَةَ، حَدَّثَنَا سَعِيدُ بْنُ سُلَيْمَانَ، عَنْ

عَبَّادٍ، عَنِ الْجُرَيْرِيِّ، عَنْ أَبِي نَضْرَةَ، عَنْ أَبِي سَعِيدٍ، قَالَ كَانَ رَسُولُ اللَّهِ

ـ صلى الله عليه وسلم ـ يَتَعَوَّذُ مِنْ عَيْنِ الْجَانِّ وَأَعْيُنِ الإِنْسِ فَلَمَّا

نَزَلَتِ الْمُعَوِّذَتَانِ أَخَذَهُمَا وَتَرَكَ مَا سِوَى ذَلِكَ .

Grade: Da'if (Darussalam)

Reference: Sunan Ibn Majah 3511
In-book Reference: Book 31, Hadith 76
English **Translation:** Vol. 4, Book 31, Hadith 3511

◆ **Narrated `Aisha (May Allah be pleased with her):**

Allah's Messenger (ﷺ) used to read in his Ruqya, "In the Name of Allah" The earth of our land and the saliva of some of us cure our patient with the permission of our Lord." with a slight shower of saliva) while treating with a Ruqya.

حَدَّثَنِي صَدَقَةُ بْنُ الْفَضْلِ، أَخْبَرَنَا ابْنُ عُيَيْنَةَ، عَنْ عَبْدِ رَبِّهِ بْنِ

سَعِيدٍ، عَنْ عَمْرَةَ، عَنْ عَائِشَةَ، قَالَتْ كَانَ النَّبِيُّ صلى الله عليه وسلم

يَقُولُ فِي الرُّقْيَةِ " تُرْبَةُ أَرْضِنَا، وَرِيقَةُ بَعْضِنَا، يُشْفَى سَقِيمُنَا، بِإِذْنِ رَبِّنَا

Reference: Sahih al-Bukhari 5746
In-book Reference: Book 76, Hadith 61
USC-MSA web (English) Reference: Vol. 7, Book 71, Hadith 642

◆ **It was narrated that 'Aisha (May Allah be pleased with her) said:**

"The Messenger of Allah (ﷺ) allowed Ruqyah for snakebites and scorpion stings."

حَدَّثَنَا عُثْمَانُ بْنُ أَبِي شَيْبَةَ، وَهَنَّادُ بْنُ السَّرِيِّ، قَالاَ حَدَّثَنَا أَبُو الأَحْوَصِ، عَنْ مُغِيرَةَ، عَنْ إِبْرَاهِيمَ، عَنِ الأَسْوَدِ، عَنْ عَائِشَةَ، قَالَتْ رَخَّصَ رَسُولُ اللَّهِ ـ صلى الله عليه وسلم ـ فِي الرُّقْيَةِ مِنَ الْحَيَّةِ وَالْعَقْرَبِ .

Grade: Sahih (Darussalam)

Reference: Sunan Ibn Majah 3517
In-book Reference: Book 31, Hadith 82
English **Translation:** Vol. 4, Book 31, Hadith 3517

◆ **Narrated Al-Aswad (May Allah be pleased with him):**

I asked `Aisha about treating poisonous stings (a snake bite or a scorpion sting) with a Ruqya. She said, "The Prophet (ﷺ) allowed the treatment of poisonous sting with Ruqya."

حَدَّثَنَا مُوسَى بْنُ إِسْمَاعِيلَ، حَدَّثَنَا عَبْدُ الْوَاحِدِ، حَدَّثَنَا سُلَيْمَانُ الشَّيْبَانِيُّ، حَدَّثَنَا عَبْدُ الرَّحْمَنِ بْنُ الأَسْوَدِ، عَنْ أَبِيهِ، قَالَ سَأَلْتُ عَائِشَةَ عَنِ الرُّقْيَةِ، مِنَ الْحُمَةِ فَقَالَتْ رَخَّصَ النَّبِيُّ صلى الله عليه وسلم الرُّقْيَةَ مِنْ كُلِّ ذِي حُمَةٍ.

Reference: Sahih al-Bukhari 5741
In-book Reference: Book 76, Hadith 56
USC-MSA web (English) Reference: Vol. 7, Book 71, Hadith 637

◆ Narrated `Aisha (May Allah be pleased with her):

Allah's Messenger (ﷺ) used to treat with a Ruqya saying, "O the Lord of the people! Remove the trouble The cure is in Your Hands, and there is none except You who can remove it (the disease). "

حَدَّثَنِي أَحْمَدُ بْنُ أَبِي رَجَاءٍ، حَدَّثَنَا النَّضْرُ، عَنْ هِشَامِ بْنِ عُرْوَةَ، قَالَ أَخْبَرَنِي أَبِي، عَنْ عَائِشَةَ، أَنَّ رَسُولَ اللَّهِ صلى الله عليه وسلم كَانَ يَرْقِي يَقُولُ " امْسَحِ الْبَاسَ رَبَّ النَّاسِ، بِيَدِكَ الشِّفَاءُ، لاَ كَاشِفَ لَهُ إِلاَّ أَنْتَ "‏.

Reference: Sahih al-Bukhari 5744
In-book Reference: Book 76, Hadith 59
USC-MSA web (English) Reference: Vol. 7, Book 71, Hadith 640

◆ **Narrated Um Salama (May Allah be pleased with her):**

The Prophet (ﷺ) saw in her house a girl whose face had a black spot. He spoke, "She is under the effect of an evil eye; so, treat her with a Ruqya."

حَدَّثَنِي مُحَمَّدُ بْنُ خَالِدٍ، حَدَّثَنَا مُحَمَّدُ بْنُ وَهْبِ بْنِ عَطِيَّةَ الدِّمَشْقِيُّ، حَدَّثَنَا مُحَمَّدُ بْنُ حَرْبٍ، حَدَّثَنَا مُحَمَّدُ بْنُ الْوَلِيدِ الزُّبَيْدِيُّ، أَخْبَرَنَا الزُّهْرِيُّ، عَنْ عُرْوَةَ بْنِ الزُّبَيْرِ، عَنْ زَيْنَبَ ابْنَةِ أَبِي سَلَمَةَ، عَنْ أُمِّ سَلَمَةَ ـ رضى الله عنها ـ أَنَّ النَّبِيَّ صلى الله عليه وسلم رَأَى فِي بَيْتِهَا جَارِيَةً فِي وَجْهِهَا سَفْعَةٌ فَقَالَ "اسْتَرْقُوا لَهَا، فَإِنَّ بِهَا النَّظْرَةَ ". وَقَالَ عُقَيْلٌ عَنِ الزُّهْرِيِّ أَخْبَرَنِي عُرْوَةُ عَنِ النَّبِيِّ صلى الله عليه وسلم. تَابَعَهُ عَبْدُ اللَّهِ بْنُ سَالِمٍ عَنِ الزُّبَيْدِيِّ.

Reference: Sahih al-Bukhari 5739
In-book Reference: Book 76, Hadith 54
USC-MSA web (English) Reference: Vol. 7, Book 71, Hadith 635

◆ Narrated Anas bin Malik (May Allah be pleased with him):

Allah's Messenger (ﷺ) allowed one of the Ansar families to treat persons who have taken poison and also who are suffering from ear ailments with Ruqya. Anas added: I got myself branded cauterized) for pleurisy, when Allah's Messenger (ﷺ) was still alive. Abu Talha, Anas bin An-Nadr and Zaid bin Thabit witnessed that, and it was Abu Talha who branded (cauterized) me.

حَدَّثَنَا عَارِمٌ، حَدَّثَنَا حَمَّادٌ، قَالَ قُرِئَ عَلَى أَيُّوبَ مِنْ كُتُبِ أَبِي قِلَابَةَ مِنْهُ مَا حَدَّثَ بِهِ وَمِنْهُ مَا قُرِئَ عَلَيْهِ، وَكَانَ هَذَا فِي الْكِتَابِ عَنْ أَنَسٍ أَنَّ أَبَا طَلْحَةَ وَأَنَسَ بْنَ النَّضْرِ كَوَيَاهُ، وَكَوَاهُ أَبُو طَلْحَةَ بِيَدِهِ. وَقَالَ عَبَّادُ بْنُ مَنْصُورٍ عَنْ أَيُّوبَ، عَنْ أَبِي قِلَابَةَ، عَنْ أَنَسِ بْنِ مَالِكٍ، قَالَ أَذِنَ رَسُولُ اللَّهِ صلى الله عليه وسلم لِأَهْلِ بَيْتٍ مِنَ الأَنْصَارِ أَنْ يَرْقُوا مِنَ الْحُمَةِ وَالأُذُنِ. قَالَ أَنَسٌ كُوِيتُ مِنْ ذَاتِ الْجَنْبِ وَرَسُولُ اللَّهِ صلى الله عليه وسلم حَيٌّ، وَشَهِدَنِي أَبُو طَلْحَةَ وَأَنَسُ بْنُ النَّضْرِ وَزَيْدُ بْنُ ثَابِتٍ، وَأَبُو طَلْحَةَ كَوَانِي.

Reference: Sahih al-Bukhari 5719, 5720, 5721
In-book Reference: Book 76, Hadith 36
USC-MSA web (English) Reference: Vol. 7, Book 71, Hadith 617

◆ **Yahya related to me from Malik from Yahya ibn Said from Amra bint Abd at-Rahman:**

Abu Bakr as-Siddiq visited A'isha while she had a [health] complaint and a Jewish woman was making incantation (ruqya) for her. Abu Bakr said, "Do it (incantation) with the Book of Allah."

وَحَدَّثَنِي عَنْ مَالِكٍ، عَنْ يَحْيَى بْنِ سَعِيدٍ، عَنْ عَمْرَةَ بِنْتِ عَبْدِ الرَّحْمَنِ، أَنَّ أَبَا بَكْرٍ الصِّدِّيقَ، دَخَلَ عَلَى عَائِشَةَ وَهِيَ تَشْتَكِي وَيَهُودِيَّةٌ تَرْقِيهَا فَقَالَ أَبُو بَكْرٍ ارْقِيهَا بِكِتَابِ اللَّهِ .

USC-MSA web (English) Reference: Book 50, Hadith 11
Arabic Reference: Book 50, Hadith 1724

◆ **Narrated Abu Huraira (May Allah be pleased with her):**

Allah's Messenger (ﷺ) ordered me to guard the Zakat

revenue of Ramadan. Then somebody came to me and started stealing from the foodstuff. I caught him and said, "I will take

you to Allah's Messenger (ﷺ)!" Then Abu Huraira described the

whole narration and said: That person said (to me), "(Please

don't take me to Allah's Messenger (ﷺ) and I will tell you a few

words by which Allah will benefit you.) When you go to your bed, recite Ayat-al-Kursi, (2.255) for then there will be a guard from Allah who will protect you all night long, and Satan will not be able to come near you till dawn." (When the Prophet (ﷺ) heard the story) he said (to me), "He (who came to you at night) told you the truth although he is a liar; and it was Satan."

وَقَالَ عُثْمَانُ بْنُ الْهَيْثَمِ حَدَّثَنَا عَوْفٌ، عَنْ مُحَمَّدِ بْنِ سِيرِينَ، عَنْ أَبِي هُرَيْرَةَ ـ رضى الله عنه ـ قَالَ وَكَّلَنِي رَسُولُ اللَّهِ صلى الله عليه وسلم بِحِفْظِ زَكَاةِ رَمَضَانَ فَأَتَانِي آتٍ فَجَعَلَ يَحْثُو مِنَ الطَّعَامِ فَأَخَذْتُهُ فَقُلْتُ لأَرْفَعَنَّكَ إِلَى رَسُولِ اللَّهِ صلى الله عليه وسلم فَقَصَّ الْحَدِيثَ فَقَالَ إِذَا أَوَيْتَ إِلَى فِرَاشِكَ فَاقْرَأْ آيَةَ الْكُرْسِيِّ لَنْ يَزَالَ مَعَكَ مِنَ اللَّهِ حَافِظٌ وَلاَ يَقْرَبُكَ شَيْطَانٌ حَتَّى تُصْبِحَ. وَقَالَ النَّبِيُّ صلى الله عليه وسلم " صَدَقَكَ وَهْوَ كَذُوبٌ ذَاكَ شَيْطَانٌ ".

Reference: Sahih al-Bukhari 5010
In-book Reference: Book 66, Hadith 32
USC-MSA web (English) Reference: Vol. 6, Book 61, Hadith 530

◆ **Narrated Abu Mas'ud (May Allah be pleased with him):**

The Prophet (ﷺ) said, "If somebody recited the last two Verses of Surat Al-Baqara at night, that will be sufficient for him."

حَدَّثَنَا أَبُو نُعَيْمٍ، حَدَّثَنَا سُفْيَانُ، عَنْ مَنْصُورٍ، عَنْ إِبْرَاهِيمَ، عَنْ عَبْدِ الرَّحْمَنِ بْنِ يَزِيدَ، عَنْ أَبِي مَسْعُودٍ ـ رضى الله عنه ـ قَالَ قَالَ النَّبِيُّ

صلى الله عليه وسلم " مَنْ قَرَأَ بِالآيَتَيْنِ مِنْ آخِرِ سُورَةِ الْبَقَرَةِ فِي لَيْلَةٍ كَفَتَاهُ".

Reference: Sahih al-Bukhari 5009
In-book Reference: Book 66, Hadith 31
USC-MSA web (English) Reference: Vol. 6, Book 61, Hadith 530

◆ **Anas (May Allah be pleased with him) reported:**

I said to Thabit (May Allah had Mercy upon him) Should I not perform Ruqyah (i.e., recite supplication or Quranic Ayat and blow) over you, such supplication as was practised by the Messenger of Allah (ﷺ)?" He said: "Please do so." Anas (May Allah be pleased with him) supplicated: "Allahumma Rabban-nasi, mudh-hibal-ba'si, ishfi Antash-Shafi, la shafiya illa Anta, shifa'an la yughadiru saqaman **[O Allah! the Rubb of mankind! Take away this disease and cure (him or her). You are the Curer. There is no cure except through You. Cure (him or her), a cure that leaves no disease].**"

وعن أنس، رضي الله عنه أنه قال لثابت رحمه الله: ألا أرقيك برقية رسول الله صلى الله عليه وسلم ؟ قال: بلى، قال: اللهُمَّ رب الناس، مذهب البأس، اشف أنت الشافي، لا شافي إلا أنت، شفاءً لا يغادر سقماً"(رواه البخاري).

[Al-Bukhari].
Reference: Riyad as-Salihin 903
In-book Reference: Book 6, Hadith 10

THE VERSES OF MANZIL

Manzil Dua is the Collection of the Following Surah Verses from The Noble Quran:

- Surah Al-Fatihah (chapter 1): verses 1 to 7
- Surah Al-Bakarah (chapter 2): verses 1 to 5, 163, 255 to 257, and 284 to 286
- Surah Al-Imran (chapter 3): verses 18, 26 and 27
- Surah Al-A'araf (chapter 7): verses 54 to 56
- Surah Al-Israa (chapter 17): verses 110 and 111
- Surah Al-Muminoon (chapter 23): verses 115 to 118
- Surah Al-Saaffaat (chapter 37): verses 1 to 11
- Surah Al-Rehman (chapter 55): verses 33 to 40
- Surah Al-Hashr (chapter 59): verses 21 to 24
- Surah Al-Jinn (chapter 72): verses 1 to 4
- Surah Al-Kaafiroon (chapter 109): verses 1 to 6
- Surah Al-Ikhlas (chapter 112): verses 1 to 4
- Surah Al-Falaq (chapter 113): verses 1 to 5
- Surah Al-Naas (chapter 114): verses 1 to 6

It was narrated from 'Abdur-Rahman bin Abi Laila that his father Abu Laila said:

"I was sitting with the Prophet (ﷺ) when a Bedouin came to him and said: 'I have a brother who is sick.' He said: 'What is the matter with your brother?' He said: 'He suffers from a slight mental derangement.' He said: 'Go and bring him.'" He said: "(So he went) and he brought him. He made him sit down in front of him and I heard him seeking refuge for him with Fatihatil-Kitab; four Verses from the beginning of Al-Baqarah, two Verses from its middle: 'And your Ilah (God) is One Ilah (God – Allah),' [2:163] and Ayat Al-Kursi; and three Verses from its end; a Verse from Al 'Imran, I think it was: 'Allah bears witness that La ilaha illa Huwa (none has the right to be worshipped but He),' [3:18] a Verse from Al-A'raf: 'Indeed, your Lord is Allah,' [7:54] a Verse from Al-Mu'minun: 'And whoever invokes (or worships), besides Allah, any other ilah (god), of whom he has no proof,'[23:117] a Verse from Al-Jinn: 'And He, exalted is the Majesty of our Lord,' [72:3] ten Verses from the beginning of As-Saffat; three Verses from the end of Al-Hashr; (then) 'Say: He is Allah, (the) One,' [112:1] and Al-Mu'awwidhatain. Then the Bedouin stood up, healed, and there was nothing wrong with him."

حَدَّثَنَا هَارُونُ بْنُ حَيَّانَ، حَدَّثَنَا إِبْرَاهِيمُ بْنُ مُوسَى، أَنْبَأَنَا عَبْدَةُ بْنُ سُلَيْمَانَ، حَدَّثَنَا أَبُو جَنَابٍ، عَنْ عَبْدِ الرَّحْمَنِ بْنِ أَبِي لَيْلَى، عَنْ أَبِيهِ أَبِي لَيْلَى، قَالَ كُنْتُ جَالِسًا عِنْدَ النَّبِيِّ ـ صلى الله عليه وسلم ـ إِذْ جَاءَهُ أَعْرَابِيٌّ فَقَالَ إِنَّ لِي أَخًا وَجِعًا . قَالَ " مَا وَجَعُ أَخِيكَ " . قَالَ بِهِ لَمَمٌ . قَالَ " اذْهَبْ فَأْتِنِي بِهِ " . قَالَ فَذَهَبَ فَجَاءَ بِهِ فَأَجْلَسَهُ بَيْنَ يَدَيْهِ فَسَمِعْتُهُ عَوَّذَهُ بِفَاتِحَةِ الْكِتَابِ وَأَرْبَعِ آيَاتٍ مِنْ أَوَّلِ الْبَقَرَةِ وَآيَتَيْنِ مِنْ وَسَطِهَا وَإِلَهُكُمْ إِلَهٌ وَاحِدٌ وَآيَةِ الْكُرْسِيِّ وَثَلَاثِ آيَاتٍ مِنْ خَاتِمَتِهَا وَآيَةٍ مِنْ آلِ عِمْرَانَ ـ أَحْسِبُهُ قَالَ }شَهِدَ اللَّهُ أَنَّهُ لاَ إِلَهَ إِلاَّ هُوَ{ ـ وَآيَةٍ مِنَ الأَعْرَافِ }إِنَّ رَبَّكُمُ اللَّهُ الَّذِي خَلَقَ{ الآيَةَ وَآيَةٍ مِنَ الْمُؤْمِنِينَ }وَمَنْ يَدْعُ مَعَ اللَّهِ إِلَهًا آخَرَ لاَ بُرْهَانَ لَهُ بِهِ { وَآيَةٍ مِنَ الْجِنِّ }وَأَنَّهُ تَعَالَى جَدُّ

رِبَّنَا مَا اتَّخَذَ صَاحِبَةً وَلاَ وَلَدَا{ وَعَشْرِ آيَاتٍ مِنْ أَوَّلِ الصَّافَاتِ وَثَلاَثِ آيَاتٍ مِنْ آخِرِ الْحَشْرِ وَ }قُلْ هُوَ اللَّهُ أَحَدٌ { وَالْمُعَوِّذَتَيْنِ . فَقَامَ الأَعْرَابِيُّ قَدْ بَرَأَ لَيْسَ بِهِ بَأْسٌ .

Grade: Da'if (Darussalam)

Reference: Sunan Ibn Majah 3549
In-book Reference: Book 31, Hadith 114
English **Translation**: Vol. 4, Book 31, Hadith 3549

Imam Hākim says: "Shaykhān (Bukhari and Muslim) have accepted the narrators of this Hadith, except for Abu Jannab al-Kalbi. But the Hadith is Mahfūz and Sahīh..."

Imam Dhahabi comments saying: "Abu Jannab al-Kalbi: Dāruqutni has said he is da`īf and the Hadith is Munkar."

And Allah Knows the Best.

Based on this hadith, along with others (Al-Bukhari, 2001: 5013, 5014, 5015, 5016, 5017, 5018; Ibn Fil, 2001: 32), all in all, there are several collections of verses that are recommended to be recited.

(1) Surah al-Fatihah (1: 1-7)

بِسْمِ ٱللَّهِ ٱلرَّحْمَٰنِ ٱلرَّحِيمِ ۝١۝

ٱلْحَمْدُ لِلَّهِ رَبِّ ٱلْعَٰلَمِينَ ۝٢۝

ٱلرَّحْمَٰنِ ٱلرَّحِيمِ ۝٣۝

مَٰلِكِ يَوْمِ ٱلدِّينِ ۝٤۝

إِيَّاكَ نَعْبُدُ وَإِيَّاكَ نَسْتَعِينُ ۝٥۝

ٱهْدِنَا ٱلصِّرَٰطَ ٱلْمُسْتَقِيمَ ۝٦۝

صِرَٰطَ ٱلَّذِينَ أَنْعَمْتَ عَلَيْهِمْ غَيْرِ ٱلْمَغْضُوبِ عَلَيْهِمْ وَلَا

ٱلضَّآلِّينَ ۝٧۝

1:1 Bi-smi-llāhi -r-raḥmāni -r-raḥīm(i)
1:2 Al-ḥamdu -li-llāhi rabbi -l-`ālamīn(a)
1:3 Ar-raḥmāni -r-raḥīm(i)
1:4 Māliki yawmi -d-dīn(i)
1:5 'Iyyāka na`budu wa-'iyyāka nasta`īn(u)

1:6 Ihdinā -ṣ-ṣirāṭa -l-mustaqīm(a)
1:7 Ṣirāṭa -l-laḏīna 'an`amta `alayhim ġayri-l-maġḍūbi
`alayhim wa-lā -ḍ-ḍāllīn(a)

Translation: In the name of Allah, Most Gracious, Most Merciful. (1) Praise be to Allah, the Cherisher and Sustainer of the worlds; (2) Most Gracious, Most Merciful; (3) Master of the Day of Judgment. (4) Thee do we worship, and Thine aid we seek. (5) Show us the straight way, (6) The way of those on whom Thou hast bestowed Thy Grace, those whose (portion) is not wrath, and who go not astray. (7)

This is the first Surah of the Qur'an, although it is not the first in the order of revelation. It was revealed to the Prophet (ﷺ) in Makkah in the early period of his mission. The Surah has seven Ayat and is both a Du'a (prayer) and an introduction to the Qur'an. It teaches the basic principles of the Islamic faith. All praise and thanks are for Allah (ﷻ) who is the Lord of all the worlds. Allah (ﷻ) is most merciful and most compassionate.

Allah (ﷻ) is also the Master of the Day of Judgement. We should pray to Allah (ﷻ) only and we should seek His help. We seek His guidance and help to walk on the straight path. This is the path of those who received Allah's favours, not the path of those who incurred His anger or who went astray.

It is understood any dua that begins with Hamd (praise) of Allah (ﷻ) is likely to be accepted and answered. The Surah begins with Hamd (praise) of Allah and it ends with a dua. The Prophet is reported to have said, "The best Dhikr is 'La ilah ila Allah' and the best dua is 'Alhamdulillah'" (Tirmidhee).

It is one of the very earliest revelations to the Prophet. We learn from authentic hadith that it was the first complete Surah that was revealed to Prophet Muhammad. Before this, only a few verses were revealed which form parts of Surah 96: al-'Alaq (The Clinging Substance) Surah 68: al-Qalam (The Pen), Surah 73: al-Muzzammil (The Enwrapped One) and Surah 74: al-Muddathir (The Cloaked One).

On the authority of Abu Hurayrah (may Allah be pleased with him) the Prophet (ﷺ), reported having quoted Allah (ﷻ) as saying: the fruits of prayer are shared equally between Me and My servant, and My servant will be granted what he asks for. As the worshipper recites [in Prayer]: "Praise be to God, the Lord of all the worlds," God will say: 'My servant has praised Me.' As he recites: "The Compassionate, the Merciful," God will say: 'My servant has thanked Me.' As he recites: "Master of the Day of Judgement," God will say: "My servant has glorified Me." As he says: "You alone do we worship, and to You alone do we turn for help," God will say: 'This is between Me and My servant, and My servant will receive what he asks for.' And, as he says: "Guide us on the straight path, the path of those on whom You have bestowed Your favours, not those who have incurred Your wrath, nor those who have gone astray," God will say: 'This is for My servant, and he will be granted his wish.' (Hadith 8, 40 Hadith Qudsi)

This ḥadīth explores some of the meanings of al-Fātiḥah. The reader will perhaps find it helpful in understanding why God has chosen this sūrah for recitation by Muslims at least seventeen times a day, as they stand up for their obligatory prayers, spread over the night and day, and even more frequently, whenever they offer voluntary prayers.

Surah al-Fatihah has a number of names:

Fatihah al-Kitab - 'Opening of the Book'
Umm al-Kitab - 'Mother of the Book'
Umm al-Qur'an - 'Mother of the Qur'an'
Sab'a al-Mathani - 'Seven oft-repeated Ayat'
Surah al-Salah - 'Surah of Prayer'
Surah ar-Ruqyah - 'Surah of Cure.'

•   Al-Fatihah (The Opening) – It is named Al-Fatihah, the Opening – because it opens the Book and by it, the recitation in prayer commences.

•   At the beginning of the Book of Tafsir, in his Sahih, Al-Bukhari said; "It is called **Umm Al-Kitab** because the Qur'an starts with it and because the prayer is started by reciting it." It was also said that it is called Umm Al-Kitab because it contains the meanings of the entire Qur'an. Ibn Jarir said, "The Arabs call every comprehensive matter that contains several specific areas an Umm. For instance, they call the skin that surrounds the brain, Umm Ar-Ra's. They also call the flag that gathers the ranks of the army an Umm." He also said, "Makkah was called Umm Al-Qura, (the mother of the Villages) because it is the grandest and the leader of all villages. It was also said that the earth was made starting from Makkah."

•   Imam Ahmad recorded that Abu Hurayrah narrated about **Umm Al-Qur'an** that the Prophet said,

هِيَ أُمُّ الْقُرْآنِ وَهِيَ السَّبْعُ الْمَثَانِي وَهِيَ الْقُرْآنُ الْعَظِيمُ

(It is Umm Al-Qur'an, the seven repeated (verses) and the Glorious Qur'an.)

- It is also named **Sab'ul-Mathani**, the Seven Oft Repeated Verses because they are frequently recited and indeed recited in every rakaah of the prayer. Allah (ﷻ) says in the Quran:

وَلَقَدْ ءَاتَيْنَٰكَ سَبْعًا مِّنَ ٱلْمَثَانِى وَٱلْقُرْءَانَ ٱلْعَظِيمَ ﴿٨٧﴾

"And We have certainly given you, seven of the often-repeated [verses] and the great Qur'an." (15:87). Surah al-Fatihah is seven Ayat.

- It is also named **Al-Hamd**, the Praise. It contains mention of hamd just as Al-Baqarah is named so because it contains mention of the cow. Some scholars also gave the reasoning that Al-Hamd comprises the heart of Al-Fatihah.

- It is named the Prayer (Al-Sharif) because its recitation is a condition for the validity of the prayer. Narrated 'Ubâdah bin As-Sâmit Allâh's Messenger said, "Whoever does not recite Sûrat Al-Fâtihah in his prayer, his prayer is invalid. (Sahih Al-Bukhâri, Vol.1, Hadîth No. 723)

The prayer is taught by Allah(ﷻ) Himself as a favour to mankind to let them know the format of prayer which is acceptable to Him. Allah (ﷻ) also responds to each segment of the prayer.

• It is also named Ash-Shifa', the Cure, due to what Ad-Darimi reports on the authority of Abu Sa'id that the Messenger of Allah (sallallahu 'alayhi wa sallam) said: "The Opening of the Book is a cure to every poison."

• It is also named Ar-Ruqya, the Spiritual Cure due to the hadith of Abu Sa'id reported by Bukhari after he had recited it to cure a person who had been bitten by a scorpion.

• Asas al-Quran (the Foundation of the Quran) – Ash-Sha'bi records on the authority of Ibn Abbas that he named it, and that he said, "The foundation of Al-Fatihah is, "Bismillah..." (with the Name of Allah, the All-Merciful, the Most Merciful.)

• Other scholars have also named it as Al-Kanz (the Treasure), Ash-Shukr (Gratitude), ad-Dua (Supplication), Ash-Shafiyah (the sufficient), Al-Kafiyah (the Sufficient), Al-Wafiyah, the Fulfillment and more.

$$\text{بِسْمِ ٱللَّهِ ٱلرَّحْمَٰنِ ٱلرَّحِيمِ ﴿١﴾}$$

(1:1) In the name of Allah, the Merciful, the Compassionate.

One of the many practices taught by Islam is that its followers should begin their activities in the name of God. This principle, if consciously and earnestly followed, will necessarily yield three beneficial results. First, one will be able to restrain oneself from many misdeeds, since the habit of pronouncing the name of God is bound to make one wonder when about to commit some offence how such an act can be reconciled with the saying of God's holy name. Second, if a man pronounces the name of God before starting good and legitimate tasks, this act will ensure that both his starting point and his mental orientation are sound. Third - and this is the most important benefit - when a man begins something by pronouncing God's name, he will enjoy God's support and succour; God will bless his efforts and protect him from the machinations and temptation of Satan. For whenever man turns to God, God turns to him as well.

(1:2) Praise be to Allah, the Lord of the entire universe.

Praise of God is the first feeling aroused in a believer's heart at the mention of God. Man's existence is an aspect of God's infinite grace, which engenders gratitude and reverence towards God. The manifestations of God's munificence and generosity to man and other creatures abound everywhere and can be seen at every moment. To praise God at the beginning and the end of every action is another fundamental principle of the Islamic faith. The Qur'ān says: "He is God; there is no deity but He. To Him belongs praise in the first and the last..." [28: 70]

Nevertheless, God's grace is such that when a believer says, 'praise be to God,' it is recorded for him as a good deed outweighing everything. `Umar ibn al-Khaṭṭāb, the Prophet's Companion, relates that the Prophet (peace be upon him) told how a man once said, "Lord, I praise You as befits the majesty of Your Face and the greatness of Your power." The two angels accompanying that man could not evaluate the remark and refer to God Almighty, who commanded them: "Register it in his record as he said it, and I shall reward him as he deserves when he returns to Me."

$$\text{اَلرَّحْمٰنِ ٱلرَّحِيمِ } \langle ٣ \rangle$$

(1:3) The Merciful, the Compassionate.

These are two attributes that encompass all meanings and aspects of mercy and compassion, and epitomise mercy as a property of God Almighty. These two attributes define the link between the Lord as Creator and His creation. It is a link based entirely on love, peace, reassurance and care, and which inspires within man a spontaneous feeling of gratitude and praise towards God. The form of the word Rahman connotes intensity. Yet God's mercy and beneficence towards His creatures are so great, so extensive and of such an infinite nature that no one word, however strong its connotation, can do it full justice. The epithet Rahim was therefore added to that of Rahman.

$$\text{مٰلِكِ يَوْمِ ٱلدِّينِ } \langle ٤ \rangle$$

(1:4) The Master of the Day of Recompense.

This verse states a fundamental Islamic principle that has a most profound influence on human life: belief in the hereafter. The Qur'ān comments on the curious fact that people have often believed in God as Creator but have failed to believe in a Day of Judgement, in a life to come, when reward and punishment are meted out to restore the balance of justice. It is about these that the Qur'ān says: "If you ask them, 'Who is it that created the heavens and the earth?' they will surely answer, 'God'" (31:25)

Elsewhere the Qur'ān says of such people: "They deem it strange that a warner should have come to them from their midst. Thus, the unbelievers say, A strange thing is this! [Are we

43

to be resurrected] after we have died and become mere dust? Such a return seems far-fetched indeed!' "(50: 2-3)

Belief in the hereafter is essential because it engages the human soul and mind and concentrates man's attention on a future existence. This in turn helps to rein in man's obsession with the present life and to transcend his immediate earthly desires. He is no longer anxious to reap all his rewards here and now; he can conquer his selfishness and develop altruistic feelings and interests. Man can go through life as a motivated, tolerant, confident and optimistic being.

إِيَّاكَ نَعْبُدُ وَإِيَّاكَ نَسْتَعِينُ ﴿٥﴾

(1:5) You alone do we worship, and You alone do we turn for help.

This verse expresses another fundamental principle that follows logically from the preceding ones. It is also a decisive and crucial principle that draws a line between the freedom man gains in submitting to God and the abuse and debasement implicit in man's servitude to man. One man has submitted himself to God and sought help and guidance from Him alone, he has achieved total liberation from the tyranny of all religious, intellectual, moral and political powers.

To the believer in Islam, human power falls into two categories: a rightly-guided power that recognises God and abides by His directions, and an arrogant, rebellious one that does not admit to God's sovereignty and authority. A Muslim is required to support and endorse the former, no matter how weak or disadvantaged it may be, and to reject and oppose the latter, regardless of its strength or dominance. The Qur'ān says: "Many a small band, by the grace of God, has vanquished a large one." (2: 249) Such victory of the apparently weaker host could only be achieved when it relies on God, the source of all power.

Islam teaches that God has created the physical world and all its forces for man's use and benefit. Man is specifically taught and directed to study the world around him, discover its potential and utilise all his environment for his good and the good of his fellow humans. Any harm that man suffers at the hands of nature is a result only of his ignorance or lack of understanding of it and the laws governing it. The more man learns about nature, the more peaceful and harmonious his relationship with nature and the environment.

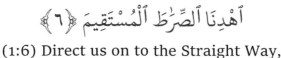

(1:6) Direct us on to the Straight Way,

With these words, a believer pleads to be shown the Right Way and to be helped along with it, which cannot be achieved without God's guidance, care and mercy. To acknowledge that is in itself a recognition of God's sovereignty and dominance over all things and events.

Guidance to the right way of life guarantees man's happiness in this world and the hereafter. It comes about, in effect, by guiding human nature and man's instincts, desires and inspirations toward the recognition and comprehension of the divine will, so bringing human activity into rhythm with the natural order and the physical world.

The sūrah reveals the nature of the "straight path" as being one taken by those whom God has favoured, not the way of those who have earned His displeasure by their deviation from the Truth, nor that of the heedless who do not know the truth. It is the path of happiness and salvation.

$$\text{صِرَاطَ ٱلَّذِينَ أَنْعَمْتَ عَلَيْهِمْ غَيْرِ ٱلْمَغْضُوبِ عَلَيْهِمْ وَلَا}$$

$$\text{ٱلضَّآلِّينَ ﴿٧﴾}$$

(1:7) The way of those whom You have favoured, who did not incur Your wrath, who are not astray.

Allah Almighty describes who are those who have the favour upon them:

$$\text{وَمَن يُطِعِ اللَّهَ وَالرَّسُولَ فَأُولَئِكَ مَعَ الَّذِينَ أَنْعَمَ اللَّهُ عَلَيْهِم مِّنَ}$$

$$\text{النَّبِيِّينَ وَالصِّدِّيقِينَ وَالشُّهَدَاءِ وَالصَّالِحِينَ ۚ وَحَسُنَ أُولَئِكَ رَفِيقًا}$$

"And whoever obeys Allah and the Messenger - those will be with the ones upon whom Allah has bestowed favour of the prophets, the steadfast affirmers of truth, the martyrs and the righteous. And excellent are those as companions." [4:69]

This makes it clear that the recipients of God's favour are not those who appear, briefly, to enjoy worldly prosperity and success; all too often, these people are among those whom God has condemned because they have lost sight of the true path of salvation and happiness. This negative explanation makes it quite clear that in'am (favour) denotes all those real and abiding favours and blessings that one receives in reward for righteous conduct through God's approval and pleasure, rather than those apparent and fleeting favours which the Pharaohs, Nimrods and Korahs (Qaruns) used to receive in the past, and which are enjoyed even today by people notorious for oppression, evil and corruption.

(2) Surah al-Baqarah (2: 1-5)

بِسْمِ ٱللَّهِ ٱلرَّحْمَٰنِ ٱلرَّحِيمِ

الٓمٓ ﴿١﴾

ذَٰلِكَ ٱلْكِتَٰبُ لَا رَيْبَ ۛ فِيهِ ۛ هُدًى لِّلْمُتَّقِينَ ﴿٢﴾

ٱلَّذِينَ يُؤْمِنُونَ بِٱلْغَيْبِ وَيُقِيمُونَ ٱلصَّلَوٰةَ وَمِمَّا رَزَقْنَٰهُمْ

يُنفِقُونَ ﴿٣﴾

وَٱلَّذِينَ يُؤْمِنُونَ بِمَآ أُنزِلَ إِلَيْكَ وَمَآ أُنزِلَ مِن قَبْلِكَ

وَبِٱلْءَاخِرَةِ هُمْ يُوقِنُونَ ﴿٤﴾

أُو۟لَٰئِكَ عَلَىٰ هُدًى مِّن رَّبِّهِمْ ۖ وَأُو۟لَٰئِكَ هُمُ ٱلْمُفْلِحُونَ ﴿٥﴾

Bismillaahir Rahmaanir Raheem.

2-1. Alif-Laaam-Meeem
2-2. Zaalikal Kitaabu laa raiba feeh; udal lilmuttaqeen
2-3. Allazeena yu'minoona bilghaibi wa yuqeemoonas salaata
wa mimmaa razaqnaahum yunfiqoon
2-4. Wallazeena yu'minoona bimaa unzila ilaika wa maaa
unzila min qablika wa bil Aakhirati hum yooqinoon
2-5. Ulaaa'ika 'alaa hudam mir rabbihim wa ulaaa'ika humul
muflihoon.

Translation: In the name of Allah (ﷻ), Most Gracious, Most

Merciful. (1) This is the Book; in it is guidance sure, without

doubt, to those who fear Allah (ﷻ); (2) Who believe in the

Unseen, are steadfast in prayer, and spend out of what We have
provided for them; (3) And who believe in the Revelation sent to
thee, and sent before thy time, and (in their hearts) have the
assurance of the Hereafter. (4) They are on (true) guidance,
from their Lord, and it is these who will prosper. (5)

(Surah al-Baqarah, 2: 1-5)

The Surah begins with the statement that it is Allah (ﷻ)

who revealed this book (the Qur'an) for the guidance of those

who are conscious of Allah (ﷻ). Only those who seek guidance

can benefit from the guidance of this Book. There are three types
of human beings:

Those who believe in the unseen realities, perform prayers,
give part of their wealth to charity, believe in what is revealed in
this scripture and what was revealed before to other prophets

and messengers of Allah (ﷻ). These are true believers. They shall benefit from this book and they shall be eternally successful.

The second group consists of those who have decided to reject Allah (ﷻ)'s message. They are the Kafirs. Since they have made up their minds to reject Islam, no preaching will help them. Allah (ﷻ) will punish them on the Day of Judgment because of their rejection.

The third is the group of people who say that they have believed, but have not believed. They try to be on both sides: sometimes on the side of faith and sometimes on the side of unfaith. They are hypocrites. They may think that in this way they will gain both sides, but in reality, they are also the losers.

The name of the Surah has been mentioned in many authentic hadeeth as 'al-Baqarah' as is mentioned by the Prophet, 'the last two Ayaat from the end of Surah al-Baqarah – whoever reads them at night it will suffice him.' [Bukhari no. 4753]

Other names used for this Surah include;
az-Zahra - The Light
as-Sanaam - The Peak
al-Fustaat - The Tent/Pavilion

al-Baqarah: This is about the story of the Cow in the incident involving the murder amongst the Children of Israel. The story of the Cow contains the most important lessons for the

Believer concerning the commands of Allah (﷾). We learn how we should and how we should not behave with respect to the Shariah and the urgency of acting upon the commands and not indulging in excessive questioning. In their implementation of the Law, their excessive questioning and hesitation in implementing the commands of Allah (﷾) led to their situation only becoming more difficult for themselves.

Sanaam: Linguistically means the peak or highest point on something or place, for example, the sanaam of a camel is in Reference to the hump being its highest point. The sanaam of a people are its leaders. Hence, Surah al-Baqarah is the peak with respect to the Qur'an as it contains the most important guidelines in establishing Islam as a system of life. The Prophet [saw] said, 'Everything has a peak and the peak of the Qur'an is al-Baqarah.' [Tirmidhee no. 2878].

Fustaat: Ibn Katheer mentions that Khalid bin Ma'dan would refer to this Surah as the fustat of the Qur'an. Fustat can be translated as 'tent' and just as the tent on the battlefield is the headquarters from which all the orders are issued, the Surah is the source/head of the remainder of the Qur'an.

Zahra: Translated as light, this Surah is a light on the path of guidance in this world and the afterlife.

The beginning of the Surah mentions the attributes of Iman [faith] that the Believer has – Ayah (2:3) and (2:4) mention Iman in:

a) al-Ghayb [unseen]
b) Belief in the Revelation sent upon Prophet Muhammad
c) Belief in the Revelations sent upon all the previous

Messengers

 d) Yaqeen [complete faith] in the Akhirah [afterlife]

 At the end of the Surah (2:285) the following aspects of Iman [faith] are mentioned:

 a) Belief in Allah (ﷻ)

 b) Belief in the Angels

 c) Belief in the Books [of revelation]

 d) Belief in the Messengers – not differentiating between any of them [their message was the same]

 Combined they form the first 5 aspects of Iman as mentioned in the Hadith of Jibril [Sahih Muslim – the only aspect of Iman not mentioned in these Ayat but said in the Hadith is Qadr.

(2:1) Alif, Lam, Mim.

 The حروف مقطعات Huruf Muqatta'at "disjointed letters" are combinations of between one and five Arabic letters appearing at the beginning of 29 out of the 114 Surahs of the Quran (approximately 33% of Surahs). A group of scholars refrained from interpreting Ayaat which contains Huruf Muqatta'at and it was not narrated that the Prophet explained them. It is preferable to say Allah (ﷻ) knows better about what they mean. However, it was narrated that some of the scholars, even amongst the Sahabah, did interpret them and they differed in their interpretation.

Ibn Kathir writes, "The individual letters at the beginning of some Surahs are among those things whose knowledge Allah (ﷻ) has kept only for Himself. This was reported from Abu Bakr, Umar, Uthman, Ali and Ibn Mas'ud. It was said that these letters are the names of some of the Surahs. The wisdom behind mentioning these letters at the beginning of the Surahs, regardless of the exact meanings of these letters, is that they testify to the miracle of the Qur'an. Indeed, the servants are unable to produce something like the Qur'an, although it is comprised of the same letters with which they speak to each other."

Initially, the Qur'an challenges all the men and jinn to produce a recital like the Qur'an and adds that they would not be able to do it even if they backed each other. This challenge is mentioned in Surah Isra (17:88) and Surah Tur (52:34). Later the Qur'an repeats the challenge in Surah Hud (11:13) by saying produce ten Surahs like it and later in Surah Yunus (10:38) produce one surah like it and finally, the easiest challenge is given in Surah Al-Baqarah (2:23).

"And if ye are in doubt as to what We have revealed from time to time to Our servant, then produce a Surah like thereunto; and call your witnesses or helpers (if there are any) besides Allah (ﷻ) if your doubts are true. But if ye cannot – and of a surety, ye cannot – then fear the Fire whose fuel is men and stones – which is prepared for those who reject faith." (2:23-24).

ذَٰلِكَ ٱلْكِتَٰبُ لَا رَيْبَ ۛ فِيهِ ۛ هُدًى لِّلْمُتَّقِينَ ﴿٢﴾

(2:2) This is the Book of Allah (ﷻ), there is no doubt in it; it is a guidance for the pious,

"This is the Scripture whereof there is no doubt": Its simple meaning is, "No doubt, this is the Book of Allah (ﷻ)", but it may also imply that this is the Book which contains nothing doubtful. It is not like the common books on metaphysics and religion which are based on mere speculation and guesswork. Therefore, even their authors cannot be free from doubts concerning their theories, despite their assertion that they are convinced of them. In contrast to them, this book is based on the Truth: its Author is He Who possesses full knowledge of Reality. Therefore, there is indeed no room for doubt about its contents.

Narrated AbuHurayrah:

The Prophet (ﷺ) said: Controverting the Qur'an is disbelief.

حَدَّثَنَا أَحْمَدُ بْنُ حَنْبَلٍ، حَدَّثَنَا يَزِيدُ، - يَعْنِي ابْنَ هَارُونَ - أَخْبَرَنَا مُحَمَّدُ بْنُ عَمْرٍو، عَنْ أَبِي سَلَمَةَ، عَنْ أَبِي هُرَيْرَةَ، عَنِ النَّبِيِّ صلى الله عليه وسلم قَالَ " الْمِرَاءُ فِي الْقُرْآنِ كُفْرٌ " .

Grade: Hasan Sahih (Al-Albani)

Reference: Sunan Abi Dawud 4603
In-book Reference: Book 42, Hadith 8
English **Translation:** Book 41, Hadith 4586

Another keyword mentioned here is 'guidance'. It expresses the essence and the nature of the Qur'ān. But guidance for whom? Who are the people who will find that this Book provides them with light, direction and true counsel? They are the God-fearing.

Once a man's heart is filled with the fear of God, he will benefit from the Qur'ān. Fear and consciousness of God is the quality that can open one's mind to the true guidance contained in the Qur'ān and allows it to have its proper effect on one's life. It is the factor that causes one's heart and mind to become sensitive and receptive to God's guidance and enables one to respond to His call and His instruction.

"a guidance unto those who ward off (evil)": That is, though there is nothing but guidance in this Book, there are a few prerequisites for benefiting from it. The first pre-requisite is that one should be inclined to avoid vice, and should seek and practise virtue. But there is no guidance in the Qur'an for the people who do not bother to consider whether what they are doing is right or wrong, who follow the ways of the world or their whims and lusts or move aimlessly in the ways of life.

$$ ٱلَّذِينَ يُؤْمِنُونَ بِٱلْغَيْبِ وَيُقِيمُونَ ٱلصَّلَوٰةَ وَمِمَّا رَزَقْنَٰهُمْ يُنفِقُونَ ﴿٣﴾ $$

(2:3) Who believe in the unseen, establish prayer, and spend out of what We have provided for them,

The most essential quality of the God-fearing believers is their conscious, active moral unity that enriches their souls with a profound belief in the imperceptible, or ghayb, dedication to their religious obligations, recognition of all God's messengers, and unshakeable certainty in the hereafter. Such are the ingredients that make the Muslim faith a complete whole and distinguish believers from unbelievers. Such a thorough outlook is worthy of God's final message to man, which was intended as a focus and a guide for all human endeavour on this earth. Man is called upon to adopt this message and lead a complete and wholesome life, guided by its light which shapes man's feelings, actions, beliefs and ways of living and behaviour.

"Who believes in the Unseen": The second condition for obtaining guidance from the Qur'an is that one must believe in the "unseen" — those realities which cannot be perceived by the senses and which do not come within human experience and observation, e.g., the essence and attributes of Allah (ﷻ),

Angels, Revelation, Heaven, Hell, etc. These things must be taken on trust from the experts (Prophets) just as we do in many cases in the physical world. Therefore, only such a person, who believes in the "unseen", can benefit from the guidance of the Qur'an. As for the one who believes only in those things which can be seen, tasted and smelt, or can be measured and weighed, cannot get any guidance from this Book.

Anas bin Malik (RA) reported that the Prophet (ﷺ) asked:

قَالَ :حَدَّثَنَا الفضل بن يعقوب الرخامي، حَدَّثنا زيد بن يَحْيَى بن عُبَيد الدمشقي، حَدَّثنا سَعِيد بْنِ بَشِيرٍ، عَن قَتادة، عَن أَنَسٍ، قَالَ :قَالَ النَّبِيّ صَلَّى اللَّهُ عَلَيه وَسَلَّم :أَيُّ الْخَلْقِ أَعْجَبُ إِيمَانًا؟ قَالُوا :الْمَلَائِكَةُ قَالَ:الْمَلَائِكَةُ كَيْفَ لَا يُؤْمِنُونَ؟ قَالَ :النَّبِيُّونَ، قَالَ:النَّبِيُّونَ يُوحَى

إِلَيْهِمْ فَكَيْفَ لَا يُؤْمِنُونَ؟قَالُوا :الصَّحَابَةُ، قَالَ:الصَّحَابَةُ يَكُونُونَ مَعَ
الْأَنْبِيَاءِ، فَكَيْفَ لا يُؤْمِنُونَ، وَلكـِن أَعْجَبُ النَّاسِ إِيمَانًا :قَوْمٌ يجيؤون
مِنْ بَعْدِكُمْ، فَيَجِدُونَ كِتَابًا مِنَ الْوَحْيِ، فَيُؤْمِنُونَ بِهِ، وَيَتَّبِعُونَهُ، فَهُمْ
أَعْجَبُ النَّاسِ، أَوِ الْخَلْقِ، إِيمَانًا

"Whose Faith (Iman) amongst the creations astounds you?"
They (the Companions) said, "The angels." He said, "The angels –
how can they not believe? (When they are with their Lord)."
They then said, "The Prophets." He said, "The Prophets receive
revelation so how would they not believe?" They then said, "The
Companions." He said, "The Companions are with the Prophets,
so how could they not believe? However, the Faith of people
which is (amazing and) astounding is those who come after you
– who find books which have been written in them, the
revelation (the Qur'ān), and hence they believe in it, (obey and)
follow it. They are the ones whose Faith is (truly) astounding."

"And establish worship": The third condition to benefit from
the Qur'an is that one should be willing and ready to put into
practice the teachings of the Qur'an. As the Salat (Prayer) is the
first and foremost obligatory duty enjoined by the Qur'an, it is
the practical proof and permanent test of the sincerity of one's
Faith. Therefore, after a person's profession of Islam, the
moment he hears the call to the Prayer (which sounds regularly
five times a day from every mosque in the Muslim world), he
should join the congregation for the Salat, because this
determines whether he is sincere in his profession or not. If he
does not attend the call and join the congregation, it is an
indication that he is not sincere in his profession. It must also be
noted that "iqama-tus-Salat: the establishment of Prayer is the
comprehensive term. It means that Salat should be performed in

56

congregation and that permanent arrangements should be made for it in every habitation; otherwise, Salat will not be considered to have been established, even if every inhabitant of a place offers the Salat individually.

"And spend of that We have bestowed upon them": The fourth condition to benefit from the Qur'an is that one should be willing to part with one's money according to the instructions of the Book to render the rights of Allah (ﷻ) and Man and should make monetary sacrifices for the cause of Islam which he has accepted.

وَٱلَّذِينَ يُؤْمِنُونَ بِمَا أُنزِلَ إِلَيْكَ وَمَا أُنزِلَ مِن قَبْلِكَ وَبِٱلْءَاخِرَةِ هُمْ يُوقِنُونَ ﴿٤﴾

(2:4) And who believe in what has been revealed to you, [O Muhammad], and what was revealed before you, and of the Hereafter, they are certain [in faith].

This is a characteristic of the Muslim community, or ummah, the rightful heir to, and custodian of, God's message and the legacy of all prophets since the dawn of human life, and the leader of mankind. This characteristic embodies such concepts as the unity of man, the oneness of God, the unity of the divine faith and God's messengers. It purges man's soul of bigotry and petty fanaticism. It reassures us of God's everlasting grace and protection which He has shown by sending successive messengers preaching one and the same faith and offering the same guidance to all mankind. It allows us to feel proud of being the recipients of God's pure and universal guidance, which remains a bright shining star that is never extinguished, even in the darkest days of human history.

"Who believe in that which is revealed unto thee (Muhammad) and that which was revealed before thee": The fifth condition is that one should believe in the truth of all those Books which Allah (ﷻ) sent down by Revelation to the Prophet Muhammad (upon whom be His peace and blessings) and the Prophets before him at different times in different countries. Those who do not believe in any kind of guidance from Allah (ﷻ), cannot at all benefit from the guidance of the Qur'an.

Likewise, those who profess to believe in the necessity of guidance from Allah (ﷻ) but do not turn to Revelation and the Prophets for it, or who dub their' own theories as "divine light", cannot obtain any guidance from it. Moreover, guidance is also denied to those who believe only in that revealed Book or Books in which their forefathers believed and reject all other guidance received from the same Source. Apart from all such people, the Qur'an guides only those who believe that they require Divine Guidance as well as admits that it does not come to every man individually but reaches humanity only through the Prophets and revealed Books. Then those who want guidance should not be slaves to any racial or national prejudices but should be seekers of truth and should submit to it wherever and in whatever form they find it.

"And are certain of the Hereafter": This is the sixth and last condition. "Hereafter" is a comprehensive word which applies to the collection of many beliefs, which are as follows: (a) Man has not been created irresponsible in the world but he is answerable to Allah (ﷻ) for all his deeds here. (b) The present world order is not everlasting but has to come to an end at a time only known to Allah (ﷻ). (c) After the present order has been brought to an

end, Allah (ﷻ) will create a new world, when He will bring

back to life all human beings, born from the beginning of creation till Resurrection, simultaneously and will call them to account for their deeds, and they will reward them justly accordingly to what they had done in the world. (d) Those, who

will be judged as good by Allah (ﷻ), will go to Paradise, and

those who will be judged as bad will be cast into Hell. (e) The criterion of success or failure is not the prosperity or adversity of this worldly life, but successful in fact will be he who comes

out successful in Allah (ﷻ)'s final judgement, and failure he

who is a failure there. Those who do not believe in the life-after-death with the above implications, cannot benefit from the Qur'an because the one who entertains' even the slightest doubt about these; not to speak of rejecting them, can never follow the way of life which the Qur'an prescribes.

$$ ﴿٥﴾ أُولَٰئِكَ عَلَىٰ هُدًى مِّن رَّبِّهِمْ ۖ وَأُولَٰئِكَ هُمُ ٱلْمُفْلِحُونَ ﴾ $$

(2:5) Such are on true guidance from their Lord; such are truly successful.

(3) Surah al-Baqarah (2: 163)

وَإِلَـٰهُكُمْ إِلَـٰهٌ وَحِدٌ لَّا إِلَـٰهَ إِلَّا هُوَ ٱلرَّحْمَـٰنُ ٱلرَّحِيمُ ﴿١٦٣﴾

2-163.Wa ilaahukum illaahunw waahid, laaa ilaaha illaa
Huwar Rahmaanur Raheem.

Translation: And your god is one God. There is no deity [worthy of worship] except Him, the Most Compassionate, the Most Merciful. (163)

(Surah al-Baqarah, 2: 163)

In the sequence of the Qur'an [not the order of Revelation] this is the first time a variation of 'La ilaha illaAllah' appears.

The oneness of God is the quintessence of faith. On the whole, the debate has never been about God's existence, however, differently his entity, attributes or role in the universe might be viewed or defined by different societies and religions. Man's nature has always led him to believe in God. The passage, therefore, affirms the principle of God's oneness as an essential part of true faith and a solid foundation for man's moral and social systems. The one God is the only deity to be adored and worshipped, and He is also the sole source of man's moral codes and norms, and the origin of all the laws and regulations that govern and control man's social, political and economic life and the life of the whole cosmos.

This central concept of Islam is re-emphasised time after time in the Qur'ān, particularly in the parts revealed in Makkah. It is brought up here in the context of preparing the Muslim community for its crucial universal leadership role. The Qur'ān hammers home these concepts so as to leave people in no doubt that the principle of God's oneness permeates all aspects of life and all parts of existence.

God's sovereignty over this world and his active control of its affairs stem from His grace attributes. He is "the Merciful, the Compassionate."

(4) Surah al-Baqarah (2: 255-257)

ٱللَّهُ لَآ إِلَـٰهَ إِلَّا هُوَ ٱلْحَىُّ ٱلْقَيُّومُ ۚ لَا تَأْخُذُهُۥ سِنَةٌ وَلَا نَوْمٌ ۚ لَّهُۥ مَا
فِى ٱلسَّمَـٰوَٰتِ وَمَا فِى ٱلْأَرْضِ ۗ مَن ذَا ٱلَّذِى يَشْفَعُ عِندَهُۥ إِلَّا
بِإِذْنِهِۦ ۚ يَعْلَمُ مَا بَيْنَ أَيْدِيهِمْ وَمَا خَلْفَهُمْ ۖ وَلَا يُحِيطُونَ بِشَىْءٍ
مِّنْ عِلْمِهِۦٓ إِلَّا بِمَا شَآءَ ۚ وَسِعَ كُرْسِيُّهُ ٱلسَّمَـٰوَٰتِ وَٱلْأَرْضَ ۖ وَلَا
يَـُٔودُهُۥ حِفْظُهُمَا ۚ وَهُوَ ٱلْعَلِىُّ ٱلْعَظِيمُ ﴿٢٥٥﴾

لَآ إِكْرَاهَ فِى ٱلدِّينِ ۖ قَد تَّبَيَّنَ ٱلرُّشْدُ مِنَ ٱلْغَىِّ ۚ فَمَن يَكْفُرْ
بِٱلطَّـٰغُوتِ وَيُؤْمِنۢ بِٱللَّهِ فَقَدِ ٱسْتَمْسَكَ بِٱلْعُرْوَةِ ٱلْوُثْقَىٰ لَا
ٱنفِصَامَ لَهَا ۗ وَٱللَّهُ سَمِيعٌ عَلِيمٌ ﴿٢٥٦﴾

ٱللَّهُ وَلِىُّ ٱلَّذِينَ ءَامَنُوا۟ يُخْرِجُهُم مِّنَ ٱلظُّلُمَـٰتِ إِلَى ٱلنُّورِ ۖ
وَٱلَّذِينَ كَفَرُوٓا۟ أَوْلِيَآؤُهُمُ ٱلطَّـٰغُوتُ يُخْرِجُونَهُم مِّنَ ٱلنُّورِ إِلَى

الظُّلُمَتِ أُوْلَئِكَ أَصْحَبُ النَّارِ هُمْ فِيهَا خُلِدُونَ ﴿٢٥٧﴾

2- 255. *Allahu laaa ilaaha illaa Huwal Haiyul Qaiyoom; laa taakhuzuhoo sinatunw wa laa nawm;*
lahoo maa fissamaawaati wa maa fil ard; man zal lazee yashfa'u indahooo illaa bi-iznih;
ya'lamu maa baina aydeehim wa maa khalfahum wa laa yuheetoona bishai'im min 'ilmihee illaa bimaa shaaa';
wasi'a Kursiyyuhus samaawaati wal arda wa laa ya'ooduho hifzuhumaa; wa Huwal Aliyyul 'Azeem.
2- 256. *Laaa ikraaha fid deeni qat tabiyanar rushdu minal ghayy; famai yakfur bit Taaghooti wa yu'mim billaahi faqadis tamsaka bil'urwatil wusqaa lan fisaama lahaa; wallaahu Samee'un 'Aleem*
2- 257. *Allaahu waliyyul lazeena aamanoo yukhrijuhum minaz zulumaati ilan noori*
wallazeena kafarooo awliyaaa'uhumut Taaghootu yukhrijoonahum minan noori ilaz KwaZulu; ulaaa'ika Ashaabun Naari hum feehaa khaalidoon.

Translation: *Allah! There is no god but He—the Living, the Self-subsisting, Eternal. Neither drowsiness overtakes Him nor sleep. To Him belongs whatever is in the heavens and whatever is on the earth. Who is it that can intercede with Him except by His permission? He knows what is [presently] before them and what will be after them, and they encompass not a thing of His knowledge except for what He wills. His Kursi extends over the heavens and the earth, and their preservation tires Him not. And He is the Most High, the Most Great. (255) There shall be no compulsion in [acceptance of] the religion. The right course has become clear from the wrong. So whoever disbelieves in Taghut and believes in Allah has grasped the most trustworthy handhold with no break in it. And Allah is Hearing and Knowing. (256) Allah is the ally of those who believe. He brings them out from* *darknesses into the light. And those who disbelieve - their allies are Taghut. They take them out of the light into darknesses. Those are the companions of the Fire; they will abide eternally therein.*

(Surah al-Baqarah, 2: 255-257)

Ayat al-Kursi is regarded as the greatest verse of the Quran according to hadith. The verse is regarded as one of the most powerful in the Quran because when it is recited, the greatness of God is believed to be confirmed. The person who recites this ayah morning and evening will be under the protection of God from the evil of the jinn and the Shaytaan (demons); this is also known as the daily adkhar.

Narrated 'Abdullah bin Mas'ud:

"Allah has not created in the heavens nor in the earth what is more magnificent than Ayat Al-Kursi." Sufyan said: "Because Ayat Al-Kursi is the Speech of Allah, and Allah's Speech is greater than Allah's creation of the heavens and the earth."

حَدَّثَنَا مُحَمَّدُ بْنُ إِسْمَاعِيلَ، قَالَ حَدَّثَنَا الْحُمَيْدِيُّ، قَالَ حَدَّثَنَا سُفْيَانُ بْنُ عُيَيْنَةَ، فِي تَفْسِيرِ حَدِيثِ عَبْدِ اللَّهِ بْنِ مَسْعُودٍ قَالَ مَا خَلَقَ اللَّهُ مِنْ سَمَاءٍ وَلاَ أَرْضٍ أَعْظَمَ مِنْ آيَةِ الْكُرْسِيِّ . قَالَ سُفْيَانُ لأَنَّ آيَةَ الْكُرْسِيِّ هُوَ كَلاَمُ اللَّهِ وَكَلاَمُ اللَّهِ أَعْظَمُ مِنْ خَلْقِ اللَّهِ مِنَ السَّمَاءِ وَالأَرْضِ .

Grade: Sahih (Darussalam)

Reference: Jami` at-Tirmidhi 2884
In-book Reference: Book 45, Hadith 10
English **Translation**: Vol. 5, Book 42, Hadith 2884

Narrated Abu Hurairah:

that the Messenger of Allah (ﷺ): "For everything, there is a hump (pinnacle) and the hump (pinnacle) of the Qur'an is Surat Al-Baqarah, in it, there is an Ayah which is the master of the Ayat in the Qur'an; [it is] Ayat Al-Kursi."

حَدَّثَنَا مَحْمُودُ بْنُ غَيْلَانَ، قَالَ حَدَّثَنَا حُسَيْنٌ الْجُعْفِيُّ، عَنْ

زَائِدَةَ، عَنْ حَكِيمِ بْنِ جُبَيْرٍ، عَنْ أَبِي صَالِحٍ، عَنْ أَبِي هُرَيْرَةَ، قَالَ

قَالَ رَسُولُ اللَّهِ صلى الله عليه وسلم " لِكُلِّ شَيْءٍ سَنَامٌ وَإِنَّ

سَنَامَ الْقُرْآنِ سُورَةُ الْبَقَرَةِ وَفِيهَا آيَةٌ هِيَ سَيِّدَةُ آيِ الْقُرْآنِ هِيَ آيَةُ

الْكُرْسِيِّ " . قَالَ أَبُو عِيسَى هَذَا حَدِيثٌ غَرِيبٌ لاَ نَعْرِفُهُ إِلاَّ مِنْ

حَدِيثِ حَكِيمِ بْنِ جُبَيْرٍ . وَقَدْ تَكَلَّمَ شُعْبَةُ فِي حَكِيمِ بْنِ

جُبَيْرٍ وَضَعَّفَهُ .

Grade: Da'if (Darussalam)

Reference: Jami` at-Tirmidhi 2878
In-book Reference: Book 45, Hadith 4
English **Translation**: Vol. 5, Book 42, Hadith 2878

Ayat-ul-Kursi Benefits:

• A Way to Seek Allah's Protection: Continuous recitation of Ayat-ul-kursi brings a person into the direct protection of Allah. Once Abu Huraira (R.A) was made in charge of Zakat revenue. During the nighttime, he had no idea as to what to do if sleep overpowers him. The Zakat revenue will be left unguarded. It was suggested to Abu Huraira (R.A), to recite Ayat-ul-Kursi and then sleep as much as he wanted to.

• Remedy for Weak Memory: If you or your kid is suffering from memory loss, you can recite this ayat and in a matter of just a few days, you will feel the change yourself. Regular recitation of Ayat-ul-Kursi whets your brain and it regains its lost potential. You can also recite this ayat for your beloved ones who have died and grant their souls, a feeling of utter solace.

• Remove All Fears: If you are afraid of someone or want to avoid the wrath of any unlucky event which seems to be coming your way, start reciting the ayat and rest assured, you will be protected be given strength by Allah to the utmost level.

اللَّهُ لَآ إِلَٰهَ إِلَّا هُوَ ٱلْحَىُّ ٱلْقَيُّومُ ۚ لَا تَأْخُذُهُۥ سِنَةٌ وَلَا نَوْمٌ ۚ لَّهُۥ مَا فِى ٱلسَّمَٰوَٰتِ وَمَا فِى ٱلْأَرْضِ ۗ مَن ذَا ٱلَّذِى يَشْفَعُ عِندَهُۥٓ إِلَّا بِإِذْنِهِۦ ۚ يَعْلَمُ مَا بَيْنَ أَيْدِيهِمْ وَمَا خَلْفَهُمْ ۖ وَلَا يُحِيطُونَ بِشَىْءٍ مِّنْ عِلْمِهِۦٓ إِلَّا بِمَا شَآءَ ۚ وَسِعَ كُرْسِيُّهُ ٱلسَّمَٰوَٰتِ وَٱلْأَرْضَ ۖ وَلَا يَـُٔودُهُۥ حِفْظُهُمَا ۚ وَهُوَ ٱلْعَلِىُّ ٱلْعَظِيمُ ﴿٢٥٥﴾

(2:255) Allah - there is no deity except Him, the Ever-Living, the Sustainer of [all] existence. Neither drowsiness overtakes Him nor sleep. To Him belongs whatever is in the heavens and whatever is on the earth. Who is it that can intercede with Him except by His permission? He knows what is [presently] before them and what will be after them, and they encompass not a thing of His knowledge except for what He wills. His Kursi extends over the heavens and the earth, and their preservation tires Him not. And He is the Most High, the Most Great.

A verse that summarises—in powerful and succinct Words— the basic principles of the Islamic faith, citing those attributes of God that most aptly assert the meaning and significance of the basic Islamic principle of tawhīd: the oneness of God.

The verse describes God as **"the Ever-Living, the Eternal Master of all"**. This implies a self-generating, self-sustaining being that is unique and independent of everything else. It is also a being without a beginning or an end, totally outside the dimension of time which defines the beginning and end of other ephemeral beings. Furthermore, this being, God Almighty, is absolute and cannot be defined in conventional terms applicable to all creation. He is unique in every respect, and nothing can be compared with Him. Thus, all other definitions or representations of God, conjured up by the human mind throughout the ages, are false and inadequate.

"The Eternal Master of all", implies that God has power over all things and that He is the supreme and ultimate cause, the raison d'etre, of everything, without whom there can be no existence or action.

The Islamic view of God gives total assurance and relates a Muslim's conscience and being, as well as everything around him, directly to God, the power that controls all existence, according to the divine scheme and order. A believer thus draws all his values, norms and standards from God's order and watches God in all his actions and behaviour.

"**Neither slumber nor sleep overtakes Him.**" This statement reinforces, in simpler and more graphic terms, the preceding one: that God is the everlasting power sustaining everything in existence. It also distinguishes God from other beings by pointing out that He is not affected by sleep to any degree, in any shape or form.

"**His is all that is in the heavens and all that is on earth.**" God's claim over the cosmos is total and absolute; unconditional and incontestable. This is another aspect of the principle of God's oneness which confirms that God is supreme, ever-present, eternal, master and owner of all. It completely invalidates the assumption that God has partners in His power or actions.

"**Who is there that can intercede with Him, except by His permission?**" This statement underlines yet another aspect of the concept of God's oneness, distinguishing clearly the Supreme Being, God, and His subordinate creation. All creatures stand in total humility and submission to the Master, never arrogating to themselves powers or authorities not delegated to them by Him. Above all, they are not to intercede on behalf of anyone without God's permission, and when they are granted such permission, they will act within its limits, as set out by God Almighty. Some will certainly attain a higher degree of approval than others, but none of them will overstep their set limits.

"**He knows all that lies open before them and all that lies hidden from them; whereas they cannot attain to anything of His knowledge save as He wills.**" This statement expresses

God's omniscience. He has total knowledge of the present, the past and the future, which human beings cannot possibly know or perceive. He is ever aware of what human beings know and what they do not, and will not, know. They can learn only what He allows them to learn.

God alone possesses full and absolute knowledge of all existence. He is able, in His infinite wisdom, to impart whatever He chooses of His knowledge to mankind, as He has promised: "We will show them Our signs in all the regions of the earth and their souls until they clearly see that this is the truth." (41: 53)

"His throne extends over the heavens and the earth, and the preservation of both does not weary Him. He is the Highest, the Greatest." Here we have another example of the unique style of the Qur'ān in expressing an abstract idea through a visual image, to make the meaning clear and accessible. The word kursī, meaning 'seat' or 'chair' and translated here as "throne", is usually used to denote the realm of sovereignty. The idea here is that God's sovereignty and authority extend over the entire cosmos, and the image makes it clear, easy to grasp and comprehend.

Likewise, the phrase, "the preservation of both does not weary Him," is an expression of God's omnipotence, depicting in simple but powerful terms how easy it is for God to sustain and preserve the heavens and the earth.

The verse ends with two more attributes of God: **"He is the Most High, the Most Great,"** exalting God above all else. The Arabic words make it clear that these attributes are exclusive to God Almighty. No human being, or any other creature, could aspire to these qualities, and those who try shall be humbled and disgraced. Elsewhere in the Qur'ān, God says: "As for the [happy] life to come, we grant it exclusively to those who seek

69

neither to exalt themselves on earth nor yet to spread corruption." (28: 83) It also castigates Pharaoh for being "a tyrant and a transgressor" (44: 31)

No matter how powerful or great a human being may grow, he can never rise above being a servant of God. Once this fact is firmly established in man's mind, it will enhance his status as subordinate to God and restrain his pride and transgression. He will truly fear God and appreciate His majesty and power and will seek to be humbler towards God and less haughty in dealing with his fellow human beings.

لَآ إِكْرَاهَ فِى ٱلدِّينِ ۖ قَد تَّبَيَّنَ ٱلرُّشْدُ مِنَ ٱلْغَيِّ ۚ فَمَن يَكْفُرْ بِٱلطَّٰغُوتِ وَيُؤْمِنۢ بِٱللَّهِ فَقَدِ ٱسْتَمْسَكَ بِٱلْعُرْوَةِ ٱلْوُثْقَىٰ لَا ٱنفِصَامَ لَهَا ۗ وَٱللَّهُ سَمِيعٌ عَلِيمٌ ﴿٢٥٦﴾

(2:256) Let there be no compulsion in religion. Truth stands out clear from Error. whoever rejects evil and believes in Allah hath grasped the most trustworthy hand-hold, that never breaks. And Allah heareth and knoweth all things.

Here again, we see how a tenet of faith is immediately translated into a code of conduct in real life. Islam looks at religious faith as a matter of conviction, once the basic facts are provided and explained. Faith is never a matter of coercion or compulsion. To achieve this conviction, Islam addresses the human being in totality. It addresses the human mind and intellect, human common sense, emotions and feelings, the innermost human nature, and the whole human conscious being. It resorts to no coercive means or physical miracles that confound the mind or that are beyond human ability to rationalise and comprehend.

By the same token, Islam never seeks converts through compulsion or threats or pressure of any kind. It deploys facts, reasoning, explanation and persuasion.

Islam came to declare and establish the great universal principle that: "There shall be no compulsion in religion. The right way is henceforth distinct from error." This reflects the honour God has reserved for a man and the high regard in which man's will, thoughts and emotions are held, the freedom he is granted to choose his beliefs, and the responsible position he is afforded to be the judge of his actions.

Freedom of belief is the most basic right that identifies man as a human being. To deny anyone this right is to deny him or her humanity. Freedom of belief also implies the freedom to express and propagate one's belief without fear of threat or persecution; otherwise, that freedom is hollow and meaningless.

The sūrah reinforces the principle with a gentle, but firm, touch to arouse the human conscience and guide it along the path of enlightenment, saying simply: "The right way is henceforth distinct from error."

The sūrah elaborates the theme further, saying: "He who rejects false deities and believes in God has indeed taken hold of the firmest support that never breaks." It is false deities that must be rejected, while faith must be reserved for God, who alone deserves faith and trust.

The Arabic term for 'false deities' is ţāghūt, meaning tyranny, a word denoting anything or anyone that takes hold of the mind or suppresses the truth, or transgresses the laws and limits set by God. It refers to forces and systems that disregard the divine religious, moral, social and legal order and operate in this life on values and principles not sanctioned by God or derived from His guidance and teachings. To resist such forces, in all their manifestations, and to believe in God's oneness is the only certain path to success and salvation.

The sūrah presents us, yet again, with another vivid image to express an abstract truth. Faith in God provides the believer with strong and unshakeable support that guarantees him certain liberation. In its essence, faith is a recognition of the most fundamental truth, the existence of God, upon which all reality stands, and an acknowledgement of the laws God has laid down for the world and by which the world exists and operates. Believers who hold to God's Guidance are assured of never drifting away from God's path or losing their way.

"God hears all and knows all." He hears what is uttered and knows what is in people's innermost souls. Those who believe in God will never be denied justice or disappointed.

Tawhid is the Most Trustworthy Handhold - Umar [ra] said, "Jibt means magic, and Taghut means Shaytan. Verily, courage and cowardice are two instincts that appear in men, the courageous fights for those whom he does not know and the coward runs away from defending his mother. Man's honour resides with his religion and his status is based upon his character, even if he was Persian or Nabatian." [Ibn Kathir]

اَللَّهُ وَلِيُّ ٱلَّذِينَ ءَامَنُوا يُخْرِجُهُم مِّنَ ٱلظُّلُمَٰتِ إِلَى ٱلنُّورِ ۖ وَٱلَّذِينَ كَفَرُوٓا أَوْلِيَآؤُهُمُ ٱلطَّٰغُوتُ يُخْرِجُونَهُم مِّنَ ٱلنُّورِ إِلَى ٱلظُّلُمَٰتِ ۗ أُوْلَٰٓئِكَ أَصْحَٰبُ ٱلنَّارِ ۖ هُمْ فِيهَا خَٰلِدُونَ ﴿٢٥٧﴾

(2:257) Allah is the Protector of those who have faith. From the depths of darkness, he will lead them forth into light. Of those who reject faith, the patrons are the evil ones: from light, they will lead them forth into the depths of darkness. They will be companions of the fire, to dwell therein (Forever).

The sūrah then goes on to present a vivid and graphic scene depicting the two paths of guidance and error. It indicates how God kindly and gently takes the believers by the hand and leads them out of the darkness, into the light, and how the false deities sponsor the unbelievers and lead them, too, by the hand, but out of the light into the darkness.

Faith is light that permeates man's soul and conscience to radiate from within his being and illuminate all things, ideas and values around him. It gives the believer a clear vision and a steady and confident understanding that enable him to identify, discern and choose. It lights his route to God, His laws and teachings, putting a man in perfect concord with the world around him. He proceeds through life in total harmony, free of all conflict and at peace with his human nature.

(5) Surah al-Baqarah (2: 284-286)

لِّلَّهِ مَا فِى ٱلسَّمَـٰوَٰتِ وَمَا فِى ٱلْأَرْضِ ۗ وَإِن تُبْدُوا۟ مَا فِىٓ
أَنفُسِكُمْ أَوْ تُخْفُوهُ يُحَاسِبْكُم بِهِ ٱللَّهُ ۖ فَيَغْفِرُ لِمَن يَشَآءُ
وَيُعَذِّبُ مَن يَشَآءُ ۗ وَٱللَّهُ عَلَىٰ كُلِّ شَىْءٍ قَدِيرٌ ﴿٢٨٤﴾
ءَامَنَ ٱلرَّسُولُ بِمَآ أُنزِلَ إِلَيْهِ مِن رَّبِّهِۦ وَٱلْمُؤْمِنُونَ ۚ كُلٌّ ءَامَنَ
بِٱللَّهِ وَمَلَـٰٓئِكَتِهِۦ وَكُتُبِهِۦ وَرُسُلِهِۦ لَا نُفَرِّقُ بَيْنَ أَحَدٍ مِّن رُّسُلِهِۦ ۚ
وَقَالُوا۟ سَمِعْنَا وَأَطَعْنَا ۖ غُفْرَانَكَ رَبَّنَا وَإِلَيْكَ ٱلْمَصِيرُ ﴿٢٨٥﴾
لَا يُكَلِّفُ ٱللَّهُ نَفْسًا إِلَّا وُسْعَهَا ۚ لَهَا مَا كَسَبَتْ وَعَلَيْهَا مَا
ٱكْتَسَبَتْ ۗ رَبَّنَا لَا تُؤَاخِذْنَآ إِن نَّسِينَآ أَوْ أَخْطَأْنَا ۚ رَبَّنَا وَلَا
تَحْمِلْ عَلَيْنَآ إِصْرًا كَمَا حَمَلْتَهُۥ عَلَى ٱلَّذِينَ مِن قَبْلِنَا ۚ رَبَّنَا وَلَا
تُحَمِّلْنَا مَا لَا طَاقَةَ لَنَا بِهِۦ ۖ وَٱعْفُ عَنَّا وَٱغْفِرْ لَنَا وَٱرْحَمْنَآ ۚ أَنتَ

مَوْلَىٰنَا فَٱنصُرْنَا عَلَى ٱلْقَوْمِ ٱلْكَٰفِرِينَ ﴿٢٨٦﴾

2-284. Lillaahi maa fissamaawaati wa maa fil ard;
wa in tubdoo maa feee anfusikum aw tukhfoohu yuhaasibkum
bihil laa;
fayaghfiru li mai yashaaa'u wa yu'azzibu mai yashaaa
u;wallaahu 'alaa kulli shai in qadeer.
2-285. Aamanar-Rasoolu bimaaa unzila ilaihi mir-Rabbihee
walmu'minoon;
kullun aamana billaahi wa Malaaa'ikathihee wa Kutubhihee wa
Rusulih
laa nufarriqu baina ahadim-mir-Rusulihee
wa qaaloo sami'naa wa ata'naa ghufraanaka Rabbanaa wa
ilaikal-maseer.
2-286. Laa yukalliful-laahu nafsan illaa wus'ahaa; lahaa maa
kasabat wa 'alaihaa maktasabat;
Rabbanaa la tu'aakhiznaa in naseenaaa aw akhtaanaa;
Rabbanaa wa laa tahmil-'alainaaa isran kamaa hamaltahoo
'alal-lazeena min qablinaa;
Rabbanaa wa laa tuhammilnaa maa laa taaqata lanaa bih
wa'fu 'annaa waghfir lanaa warhamnaa;
Anta mawlaanaa fansurnaa 'alal qawmil kaafireen.

Translation: To Allah belongs whatever is in the heavens and whatever is in the earth. Whether you show what is within yourselves or conceal it, Allah will bring you to account for it. Then He will forgive whom He wills and punish whom He wills, and Allah is over all things competent. (284) The Messenger has believed in what was revealed to him from his Lord, and [so have] the believers. All of them have believed in Allah and His angels and His books and His messengers, [saying], "We make no distinction between any of His messengers." And they say,

"We hear and we obey. [We seek] Your forgiveness, our Lord, and to You is the [final] destination."(285) Allah does not charge a soul except [with that within] its capacity. It will have [the consequence of] what [good] it has gained, and it will bear [the consequence of] what [evil] it has earned. "Our Lord, do not impose blame upon us if we have forgotten or erred. Our Lord, and lay not upon us a burden like that which You laid upon those before us. Our Lord, and burden us not with that which we have no ability to bear. And pardon us, and forgive us, and have mercy upon us. You are our protector, so give us victory over the disbelieving people."(286)

(Surah al-Baqarah, 2: 284-286)

The sūrah goes on to elaborate this point further, arousing deeper fear and consciousness of God, to whom everything belongs and who is aware of every thought, whether concealed or stated. He is sure to bring everyone to account, and He has full control over people's ultimate destiny.

One of the most distinctive features of the Qur'ānic legislative approach is that it combines purely legalistic directives with emotional and spiritual exhortations. Thus, it links the rules to be implemented in human life to their source, the Creator of all life, within a context-rich with fear of, and hope in, God Almighty. Islam moulds individual hearts and souls, as well as society as a whole, to which it addresses its legislation to achieve perfect harmony between morality and law, piety and authority. It is a code of life designed and laid down for man by his Creator, which can never be rivalled by anything that man, with his limited knowledge, perception and life duration, can ever hope to produce or achieve. After all, human beings always differ in their views and perspectives. Why, then, does humanity try to run away from its Creator who knows best what suits His creation in every case, time or situation?

Allah states that His is the kingship of the heavens and earth and of what and whoever is on or between them, that He has perfect watch over them. No apparent matter or secret that the heart conceals is ever a secret to Him, however minor it is. Allah also states that He will hold His servants accountable for what they do and what they conceal in their hearts.

When this Ayat was revealed to the Messenger of Allah, it was very hard for the Companions of the Messenger. The Companions came to the Messenger and fell to their knees saying, `O Messenger of Allah! We were asked to perform what we can bear of deeds: the prayer, the fast, Jihad and charity. However, this Ayah was revealed to you, and we cannot bear it.' The Messenger of Allah said,

أَتُرِيدُونَ أَنْ تَقُولُوا كَما قَالَ أَهْلُ الْكِتَابَيْنِ مِنْ قَبْلِكُمْ : سَمِعْنَا وَعَصَيْنَا؟ بَلْ قُولُوا : سَمِعْنَا وَأَطَعْنَا غُفْرَانَكَ رَبَّنَا وَإِلَيْكَ الْمَصِيرِ

"Do you want to repeat what the People of the Two Scriptures before you said, that is, `We hear and we disobey' Rather, say, `We hear and we obey, and we seek Your forgiveness, O our Lord, and the Return is to You?" When the people accepted this statement and their tongues recited it, Allah sent down afterwards,

ءَامَنَ الرَّسُولُ بِمَآ أُنزِلَ إِلَيْهِ مِن رَّبِّهِ وَالْمُؤْمِنُونَ كُلٌّ ءَامَنَ بِاللَّهِ وَمَلَئِكَتِهِ وَكُتُبِهِ وَرُسُلِهِ لاَ نُفَرِّقُ بَيْنَ أَحَدٍ مِّن رُّسُلِهِ وَقَالُواْ سَمِعْنَا وَأَطَعْنَا غُفْرَانَكَ رَبَّنَا وَإِلَيْكَ الْمَصِيرُ

77

"The Messenger believes in what has been sent down to him from his Lord, and (so do) the believers. Each one believes in Allah, His Angels, His Books, and His Messengers. (They say,) "We make no distinction between one another of His Messengers - and they say, "We hear, and we obey. (We seek) Your forgiveness, our Lord, and to You is the return (of all)." When they did that, Allah abrogated the Ayah 2:284 and sent down the Ayah,

$$ لاَ يُكَلِّفُ اللَّهُ نَفْسًا إِلاَّ وُسْعَهَا لَهَا مَا كَسَبَتْ وَعَلَيْهَا مَا ا كْتَسَبَتْ $$

$$ رَبَّنَا لاَ تُؤَاخِذْنَآ إِن نَّسِينَآ أَوْ أَخْطَأْنَا $$

"Allah burdens not a person beyond his scope. He gets a reward for that (good) which he has earned, and he is punished for that (evil) which he has earned. "Our Lord! Punish us not if we forget or fall into error.") until the end." [Quoted by Ibn Kathir]

Imam Ahmad recorded that Mujahid said, "I saw Ibn `Abbas and said to him, `O Abu Abbas! I was with Ibn `Umar, and he read this Ayah and cried.' He asked, `Which Ayah' I said,

$$ وَإِن تُبْدُواْ مَا فِي أَنفُسِكُمْ أَوْ تُخْفُوهُ $$

"And whether you disclose what is in yourselves or conceal it." Ibn `Abbas said, `When this Ayah was revealed, it was very hard on the Companions of the Messenger of Allah and worried them tremendously. They said: O Messenger of Allah! We know that we would be punished according to our statements and our actions, but as for what occurs in our hearts, we do not control what is in them.' The Messenger of Allah said,

$$ قُولُوا :سَمِعْنَا وَأَطَعْنَا $$

"Say, `We hear and we obey.'" They said, `We hear and we obey.' Thereafter, this Ayah abrogated the previous Ayah,

"ءَامَنَ الرَّسُولُ بِمَآ أُنزِلَ إِلَيْهِ مِن رَّبِّهِ وَالْمُؤْمِنُونَ كُلٌّ ءَامَنَ بِاللَّهِ"

The Messenger believes in what has been sent down to him from his Lord, and (so do) the believers. Each one believes in Allah), until,

لَا يُكَلِّفُ اللَّهُ نَفْسًا إِلَّا وُسْعَهَا لَهَا مَا كَسَبَتْ وَعَلَيْهَا مَا اكْتَسَبَتْ

"Allah burdens not a person beyond his scope. He gets reward for that (good) which he has earned, and he is punished for that (evil) which he has earned." Therefore, they were pardoned what happens in their hearts, and were held accountable only for their actions."

It was narrated that 'Abdullah said:

"When the Messenger of Allah (ﷺ) was taken on the Night Journey, he came to Sidrah Al-Muntaha, which is in the sixth heaven. That is where everything that comes up from below ends, and where everything that comes down from above until it is taken from it. Allah says: When what covered the lote-tree did cover it! [1] He said: "It was moths of gold. And I was given three things: The five daily prayers, the last verses of Surah Al-Baqarah, and whoever of my Ummah die without associating anything with Allah will be forgiven for Al-Muqhimat." [2]

[1] An-Najm 53:16.
[2] "The sins of the worst magnitude that drag one into the Fire." (An-Nihayah)

أَخْبَرَنَا أَحْمَدُ بْنُ سُلَيْمَانَ، قَالَ حَدَّثَنَا يَحْيَى بْنُ آدَمَ، قَالَ حَدَّثَنَا

مَالِكُ بْنُ مِغْوَلٍ، عَنِ الزُّبَيْرِ بْنِ عَدِيٍّ، عَنْ طَلْحَةَ بْنِ مُصَرِّفٍ، عَنْ

مُرَّةَ، عَنْ عَبْدِ اللَّهِ، قَالَ لَمَّا أُسْرِيَ بِرَسُولِ اللَّهِ صلى الله عليه وسلم

انْتُهِيَ بِهِ إِلَى سِدْرَةِ الْمُنْتَهَى وَهِيَ فِي السَّمَاءِ السَّادِسَةِ وَإِلَيْهَا يَنْتَهِي مَا

عُرِجَ بِهِ مِنْ تَحْتِهَا وَإِلَيْهَا يَنْتَهِي مَا أُهْبِطَ بِهِ مِنْ فَوْقِهَا حَتَّى يُقْبَضَ مِنْهَا

قَالَ } إِذْ يَغْشَى السِّدْرَةَ مَا يَغْشَى { قَالَ فَرَاشٌ مِنْ ذَهَبٍ فَأُعْطِيَ ثَلاَثًا

الصَّلَوَاتُ الْخَمْسُ وَخَوَاتِيمُ سُورَةِ الْبَقَرَةِ وَيُغْفَرُ لِمَنْ مَاتَ مِنْ أُمَّتِهِ لاَ

يُشْرِكُ بِاللَّهِ شَيْئًا الْمُقْحِمَاتُ .

Grade: Sahih (Darussalam)

Reference: Sunan an-Nasa'i 451
In-book Reference: Book 5, Hadith 4
English **Translation**: Vol. 1, Book 5, Hadith 452

ءَامَنَ ٱلرَّسُولُ بِمَآ أُنزِلَ إِلَيْهِ مِن رَّبِّهِ وَٱلْمُؤْمِنُونَ كُلٌّ ءَامَنَ

بِٱللَّهِ وَمَلَٰئِكَتِهِ وَكُتُبِهِ وَرُسُلِهِ لَا نُفَرِّقُ بَيْنَ أَحَدٍ مِّن رُّسُلِهِ

وَقَالُوا۟ سَمِعْنَا وَأَطَعْنَا غُفْرَانَكَ رَبَّنَا وَإِلَيْكَ ٱلْمَصِيرُ ﴿٢٨٥﴾

(2:285) The Messenger believeth in what hath been revealed
to him from his Lord, as do the men of faith. Each one (of them)
believeth in Allah, His angels, His books, and His messengers.
"We make no distinction (they say) between one and another of
His messengers." And they say: "We hear, and we obey: (We

seek) Thy forgiveness, our Lord, and to Thee is the end of all journeys."

The Messenger's faith springs directly from the revelations he receives from God, the ultimate truth. It is a degree of faith that cannot be described except by one who has experienced it; it remains beyond comprehension for those mortals who have not experienced divine revelation and is, therefore, unique and exclusive to God's Messenger himself. That is why it is such an honour for ordinary believers to be mentioned side by side with God's Messenger.

"Each one of them believes in God..." According to Islam, belief in God is the foundation of a Muslim's understanding of life, and the code governing his life, morals, economics and all other activities. It means believing in God as the Supreme Being, the Lord of everything and the sole object of reverence and worship. He is the ultimate authority over man's conscience and behaviour in every single aspect of his life.

"... and His angels..." This is an important aspect of belief in the unseen, which lies beyond human perception or understanding, or, to use the Islamic term ghayb, as already discussed at the beginning of the sūrah. Man's ability to perceive and accept a world above and beyond the physical world whose existence he can discern and verify sets him above the rest of creation and confers on him his human qualities. This belief puts into proper perspective man's natural curiosity for what lies beyond the material physical world, which he instinctively and perceives to exist. Without this clear perspective and vision, man resorts to myth and superstition, leading to imbalance and instability.

"… **and His books and His messengers. We make no distinction between any of His messengers**." According to the Islamic view, belief in God's books and messengers follows logically and naturally from belief in God Himself. To believe in God is to believe in the truth of all that is revealed by Him, in the honour and integrity of all the messengers He has commissioned, and in the unity of the source of the messages, they have preached. A Muslim has no notion of discrimination between God's messengers. They all preached Islam in various versions, suited to the circumstances of the communities they addressed. Muḥammad, (peace be upon him), was the last and final of those Prophets and messengers who delivered the final, complete and universal version of Islam, which will remain valid for the rest of time.

Those who truly believe in God and His angels, books and messengers, know well that they shall return to their Lord, and so they turn to Him in obedience and submission, seeking His mercy and forgiveness. "And they say, 'We hear and we obey. Grant us Your forgiveness, our Lord; to You, we shall all return.'"

With submission and obedience to the Lord comes a feeling of inadequacy and deficiency in paying one's dues to God. Thus, believers appeal to the merciful God to overlook their failures and shortcomings: "… **Grant us Your forgiveness, our Lord**…"

The appeal for forgiveness follows the assertion of total submission and obedience. It is then followed by certainty in one's fate here in this life and in the life to come. God's word is the final and ultimate truth; everything shall return to Him; He is omnipotent; His will is done and His power unchallenged; His forgiveness, mercy and grace provide the way to escape punishment for sins we commit.

"To You, we shall all return." This statement implies belief in the hereafter, which, from the Islamic point of view, is another essential aspect of faith in God. Islam asserts that God has created man and made him His vicegerent on earth based on a clear covenant encompassing all man's activities on earth. Throughout his earthly existence, man is on probation. When his probation is over, he shall be judged and made accountable for his actions. Thus, belief in the Day of Judgement and man's accountability for his deeds is a correlative of belief in God. This faith plays a central role in shaping and guiding a believer's conscience and behaviour, and his perception of values and consequences in this life.

This short Qur'ānic verse encapsulates the basic concept of the unity and integrity of Islamic belief. It is a simple and clear belief in the unity of God, His angels, His books and messengers, with no distinction among those messengers whatsoever, based on total obedience and submission to God and unshakeable faith in the Day of Judgement.

لَا يُكَلِّفُ ٱللَّهُ نَفْسًا إِلَّا وُسْعَهَا ۚ لَهَا مَا كَسَبَتْ وَعَلَيْهَا مَا ٱكْتَسَبَتْ ۗ رَبَّنَا لَا تُؤَاخِذْنَا إِن نَّسِينَا أَوْ أَخْطَأْنَا ۚ رَبَّنَا وَلَا تَحْمِلْ عَلَيْنَا إِصْرًا كَمَا حَمَلْتَهُ عَلَى ٱلَّذِينَ مِن قَبْلِنَا ۚ رَبَّنَا وَلَا تُحَمِّلْنَا مَا لَا طَاقَةَ لَنَا بِهِ ۦ ۖ وَٱعْفُ عَنَّا وَٱغْفِرْ لَنَا وَٱرْحَمْنَا ۚ أَنتَ مَوْلَىٰنَا فَٱنصُرْنَا عَلَى ٱلْقَوْمِ ٱلْكَٰفِرِينَ ﴿٢٨٦﴾

(2:286) On no soul doth Allah Place a burden greater than it can bear. It gets every good that it earns, and it suffers every ill that it earns. (Pray:) "Our Lord! Condemn us not if we forget or fall into error; our Lord! Lay not on us a burden Like that which Thou didst lay on those before us; Our Lord! Lay not on us a burden greater than we have the strength to bear. Blot out our sins, and grant us forgiveness. Have mercy on us. Thou art our Protector; Help us against those who stand against faith."

The sūrah ends with the ayat: "**God does not charge a soul with more than it can bear. In its favour shall be whatever good it does, and against whatever evil it does.**" It is within this framework of divine mercy and justice that a Muslim views, with total confidence and satisfaction, his obligations as God's vicegerent on earth, the challenges he faces in fulfilling those obligations, and the ultimate reward he receives. He is content in the belief that God is fully aware of his abilities and limitations, and will not overburden him or subject him to any duress or coercion. Not only does this fill a believer's heart with contentment and peace of mind, but it also inspires him to discharge his duties to the best of his ability. He is fully aware that any weakness he may experience is not because the task is excessive, but due to his shortcomings, and this, in turn, motivates him to strengthen his resolve and strive for excellence in his actions.

The second part of the statement emphasises individual responsibility for action: "... **In its favour shall be whatever good it does, and against whatever evil it does.**" Every individual is accountable for their actions. No responsibility can be transferred from one person to another, nor can any person come to the aid of another in the matter of accountability. Once people appreciate this principle, each and every one of them becomes a positive and active force in society. They become responsible human beings ready to defend God's right over them, unwilling to concede it to anyone else. They will resist submission to temptation, tyranny, transgression and corruption, and submit their whole physical and spiritual being to God Almighty. Those who give in to powers other than God's, except those people subjected to duress or coercion, have only themselves to blame and shall have to face the full consequences of their actions.

On the Day of Judgement, no one shall intercede on behalf of anyone else, and everyone shall stand alone to face God's judgement. This inspires healthy individualism, spurring every member of society to fulfil his or her obligations towards the community, which derive from their obligations towards God. Individuals are obliged to share their wealth, labour and wisdom, and the responsibility to bring about good and fight evil and falsehood, and earn their respective rewards individually and directly from God Almighty.

As the believers understand and appreciate the significance and implications of these principles, they make their earnest plea to God. The Qur'ān, in its fine and highly expressive style, quotes their moving, passionate prayer. The reader can almost see the multitudes of believers reciting in unison throughout the generations this prayer, evoked by a dual feeling of hope and fear: **"Our Lord, do not take us to task if we forget or unwittingly do wrong. Our Lord, do not lay on us a burden such as that You laid on those before us. Our Lord, do not burden us with what we do not have the strength to bear. Pardon us, forgive us our sins, and bestow Your mercy on us. You are our Lord Supreme; grant us victory against the unbelievers."**

It is a prayer that clearly defines the relationship between the believers and their Lord. In its soft tone and poignant rhythm, it implies an admission of weakness and helplessness, and a recognition of the need for God's aid, support, forgiveness and grace.

"**Our Lord, do not take us to task if we forget or unwittingly do wrong.**" Error and forgetfulness are two defining characteristics of human behaviour. In recognition of this, a Muslim never boasts of his faults, nor deliberately exploits them, or places himself above God's will, but always seeks God's help and turns to Him in repentance. The answer to this prayer is given by the Prophet who says: "**God has pardoned my followers anything they do through a genuine mistake, forgetfulness or by compulsion.**" [Related by al-Ṭabarānī and others]

"**Our Lord, do not lay on us a burden such as that You laid on those before us.**" This plea stems from an appreciation of the gravity of the responsibility placed upon the Muslim community as heirs and custodians of God's message to mankind. It also reflects full absorption of the lessons and experiences of earlier nations who had received God's revelations, as related in the Qur'ān. We have seen, for example, earlier in this sūrah that the Israelites were castigated and penalised on several occasions, and in various ways, for their stubbornness and intransigence. Elsewhere in the Qur'ān, we read that, for similar reasons, they were forbidden certain foods: "**To those who followed the Jewish faith did We forbid all animals that have claws; and We forbade them the fat of both oxen and sheep, except that which is in their backs and entrails and what is mixed with their bones. Thus, did We requite them for their wrongdoing?**" (6:146) On a certain occasion, they were ordered to kill one another in atonement for their worship of the calf, as stated in Verse 54 of this sūrah. They were also forbidden to conduct any business or to hunt on the Sabbath.

Hence, believers appeal to God not to burden them in the same way as He imposed on earlier communities. The Prophet Muḥammad was sent with a tolerant and benevolent religion that is fully cognizant of human nature and is aimed at relieving mankind of all the burdens and encumbrances placed upon them. The Prophet is told by God: **"We shall smooth your way to perfect ease."** (87:8)

"Our Lord, do not burden us with what we do not have the strength to bear." This is not an excuse for negligence or a justification for dereliction of duty, but a plea by the weak to the powerful, for consideration and forbearance. A conscientious believer does not wish to fail in serving his Lord and Creator, and so he asks for leniency and tolerance. While acknowledging his weakness, a true believer remains vigilant and tries to compensate for his shortcomings by seeking more of God's grace and forgiveness.

"Pardon us, and forgive us our sins, and bestow Your mercy on us." This is the only true guarantee of success and deliverance. No matter how hard a man strives to live up to his obligations and responsibilities towards God, he will not fulfil them satisfactorily. God shows grace by treating a man with mercy and forgiveness. A'ishah, the Prophet's wife, reported that the Prophet had said, **"No man shall enter Paradise by virtue of his deeds alone."** When asked, **"How about you?"** he replied, **"Not even I, unless God bestows mercy on me."** [Related by al-Bukhārī]

The sūrah closes with a statement asserting that believers put their full trust in God to come to their help in establishing His order on earth and defending it against its foes. God is the source of their strength and their ultimate triumph.

"You are our Lord Supreme; grant us victory against the unbelievers." These words encapsulate the essence of the sūrah as well as the faith of Islam. They reflect the mind of true believers and define the eternal relationship between them and their Supreme Lord.

(6) Surah Ali 'Imran (3: 18)

شَهِدَ ٱللَّهُ أَنَّهُۥ لَآ إِلَٰهَ إِلَّا هُوَ وَٱلْمَلَٰٓئِكَةُ وَأُوْلُواْ ٱلْعِلْمِ قَآئِمًا
بِٱلْقِسْطِ ۚ لَآ إِلَٰهَ إِلَّا هُوَ ٱلْعَزِيزُ ٱلْحَكِيمُ ﴿١٨﴾

*3-18. Shahidal laahu annahoo laa ilaaha illaa Huwa
walmalaaa'ikatu wa ulul 'ilmi qaaa'imam bilqist;
laaa ilaaha illaa Huwal 'Azeezul Hakeem.*

Translation: *Allah witnesses that there is no deity except
Him, and [so do] the angels and those of knowledge - [that He is]
maintaining [creation] injustice. There is no deity except Him, the
Exalted in Might, the Wise. (18)*

Surah Ali 'Imran [3:18]

This chapter is named after the family of Imran, which
includes Imran, his wife, Mariam, and Isa.

Abu Umama said he heard Allah's Messenger (ﷺ) say:

Recite the Qur'an, for on the Day of Resurrection it will come
as an intercessor for those who recite It. Recite the two bright
ones, al-Baqara and Surah Al 'Imran, for on the Day of
Resurrection they will come as two clouds or two shades, or two
flocks of birds in ranks, pleading for those who recite them.
Recite Surah al-Baqara, for to take recourse to it is a blessing
and to give it up is a cause of grief, and the magicians cannot
confront it. (Mu'awiya said: It has been conveyed to me that here
Batala means magicians.)

حَدَّثَنِي الْحَسَنُ بْنُ عَلِيٍّ الْحُلْوَانِيُّ، حَدَّثَنَا أَبُو تَوْبَةَ، - وَهُوَ الرَّبِيعُ

بْنُ نَافِعٍ - حَدَّثَنَا مُعَاوِيَةُ، - يَعْنِي ابْنَ سَلاَّمٍ - عَنْ زَيْدٍ، أَنَّهُ سَمِعَ أَبَا

سَلاَّمٍ، يَقُولُ حَدَّثَنِي أَبُو أُمَامَةَ، الْبَاهِلِيُّ قَالَ سَمِعْتُ رَسُولَ اللَّهِ

صلى الله عليه وسلم يَقُول " اقْرَءُوا الْقُرْآنَ فَإِنَّهُ يَأْتِي يَوْمَ الْقِيَامَةِ

شَفِيعًا لأَصْحَابِهِ اقْرَءُوا الزَّهْرَاوَيْنِ الْبَقَرَةَ وَسُورَةَ آلِ عِمْرَانَ فَإِنَّهُمَا

تَأْتِيَانِ يَوْمَ الْقِيَامَةِ كَأَنَّهُمَا غَمَامَتَانِ أَوْ كَأَنَّهُمَا غَيَايَتَانِ أَوْ

كَأَنَّهُمَا فِرْقَانِ مِنْ طَيْرٍ صَوَافَّ تُحَاجَّانِ عَنْ أَصْحَابِهِمَا اقْرَءُوا

سُورَةَ الْبَقَرَةِ فَإِنَّ أَخْذَهَا بَرَكَةٌ وَتَرْكَهَا حَسْرَةٌ وَلاَ تَسْتَطِيعُهَا الْبَطَلَةُ

. قَالَ مُعَاوِيَةُ بَلَغَنِي أَنَّ الْبَطَلَةَ السَّحَرَةُ . "

Reference: Sahih Muslim 804a
In-book Reference: Book 6, Hadith 302
USC-MSA web (English) Reference: Book 4, Hadith 1757

The oneness of God and that He is the Eternal Master of the universe—who maintains and executes justice. It is the same principle with which this sūrah opens: "**God: there is no deity save Him, the Ever-living, the Eternal Master of all.**" The ultimate objective of this sūrah is to establish in absolute clarity the true nature of the Islamic faith and to dispel all doubts about it raised by people of earlier revelations. It seeks to dispel such doubts both from the minds of those unbelievers and also from the minds of those Muslims who may fall under their influence.

The testimony of the angels and the people of knowledge takes the form of their total obedience to God's orders and looking to Him alone for guidance, accepting everything which comes to them from Him without doubt or argument, once they are certain that it has come from Him. This sūrah has already referred to the attitude of such people of knowledge: "Those who are firmly grounded in knowledge say: 'We believe in it; it is all from our Lord." This is, then, the testimony of the people of knowledge and the angels: total acceptance, obedience and submission.

The testimony of God, the angels and the men of knowledge to the oneness of God is coupled with their testimony to the fact that He establishes and maintains justice since justice is an essential quality of the Godhead. The Arabic text is phrased in such a way as to leave no doubt that justice, at all times and in all situations, is an attribute of God. This also explains the meaning of God being the Eternal Master of the universe which is stated at the beginning of this sūrah: "God: there is no deity save Him, the Ever-living, the Eternal Master of all." He maintains His authority with justice.

"There is no deity save Him, the Almighty, the Wise." The same truism of the Oneness of God has been repeated in the same verse, but this time it is coupled with the two attributes of God's might and wisdom. Both power and wisdom are essential for the purpose of maintaining justice. Justice can only be maintained when matters are set in their proper places and with the ability to so set them. God's attributes suggest positive activity. Nothing in the Islamic concept associates God with any negative attribute. This is the proper and true concept of the Divine Being because it is His own description of Himself. When we believe in God, in the light of His positive attributes, our thoughts remain concentrated on His will and His power. Our faith, then, becomes much more than an academic concept; it provides us with a dynamic motive to act and do what is required of us.

(7) Surah Ali ‘Imran (3: 26-27)

قُلِ ٱللَّهُمَّ مَٰلِكَ ٱلْمُلْكِ تُؤْتِى ٱلْمُلْكَ مَن تَشَآءُ وَتَنزِعُ ٱلْمُلْكَ
مِمَّن تَشَآءُ وَتُعِزُّ مَن تَشَآءُ وَتُذِلُّ مَن تَشَآءُ ۖ بِيَدِكَ ٱلْخَيْرُ ۖ إِنَّكَ
عَلَىٰ كُلِّ شَىْءٍ قَدِيرٌ ﴿٢٦﴾
تُولِجُ ٱلَّيْلَ فِى ٱلنَّهَارِ وَتُولِجُ ٱلنَّهَارَ فِى ٱلَّيْلِ ۖ وَتُخْرِجُ ٱلْحَىَّ مِنَ
ٱلْمَيِّتِ وَتُخْرِجُ ٱلْمَيِّتَ مِنَ ٱلْحَىِّ ۖ وَتَرْزُقُ مَن تَشَآءُ بِغَيْرِ
حِسَابٍ ﴿٢٧﴾

*3-26. Qulil laahumma Maalikal Mulki tu'til mulka man
tashaaa'u
wa tanzi'ulmulka mimman tashhaaa'u wa tu'izzu man
tashaaa'u
wa tuzillu man tashaaa'u biyadikal khairu innaka 'alaa kulli
shai'in Qadeer.
3-27. Toolijul laila fin nahaari wa toolijun nahaara fil laili
wa tukhrijul haiya minalmaiyiti wa tukhrijulo
maiyita minal haiyi wa tarzuqu man tashaaa'u bighari hisab.*

93

Translation: Say, "O Allah, Owner of Sovereignty, you give sovereignty to whom You will and You take sovereignty away from whom You will. You honour whom You will and You humble whom You will. In Your hand is [all] good. Indeed, you are overall things competent. (26) You cause the night to enter the day, and You cause the day to enter the night, and You bring the living out of the dead, and You bring the dead out of the living. And You give provision to whom You will without an account."(27)

Surah Ali 'Imran [3: 26-27]

(3: 26) This expresses the natural result of the oneness of God. Since there is only a single deity, He is then the only Master, **"the Sovereign of all dominion"** Who has no partners. He gives whatever portion He wishes of His dominion to whomever He wants of His servants. What is given becomes simply like a borrowed article. Its owner retains his absolute right of taking it back whenever he wants. No one, then, has any claim of original dominion giving him the right of absolute power. It is simply a received dominion, subject to the terms and conditions stipulated by the original Sovereign. If the recipient behaves in any way which constitutes a violation of these conditions, his action is invalid. Believers have a duty to stop him from that violation in this life. In the life to come, he will have to account for his violation of the terms stipulated by the original Sovereign.

He is also the One Who exalts whom He wills and abases whom He wills. He needs no one to ratify His judgement. No one grants protection against the will of God, and no one has the power to prevent His will from taking its full course. His power is absolute and His control is total.

The authority of God ensures the realisation of all goodness. He exercises it with justice. When He gives dominion to anyone or takes it away from him, He does so with justice. Similarly, it is with justice that He exalts or abases any of His servants. This ensures real goodness, in all situations. It is sufficient that He should something for it to be realised: **"In Your hand is all that is good. You are able to do all things."**

(3: 26) Some commentators explain that what is meant by the night and day passing into each other is that each of them takes part of the other when one of the four seasons succeeds another. Others believe that it refers to each of them creeping into the other with the first shades of darkness every evening and the first rays of light every morning.

Whichever explanation we prefer, our hearts can almost visualise God's hand as it works in the universe wrapping one ball in darkness and opening another to daylight, reversing one position into another. We can see the dark lines gradually creeping into the light of day, and we can see the dawn slowly beginning to breathe, with the darkness all around. The night stretches little by little as it gains more and more of the hours of the day at the beginning of winter, and the day stretches little by little, gaining on the night, as summer approaches. No man ever claims to control either movement with its fine subtleties. No rational person can ever claim that either movement happens by chance.

The same applies to the cycle of life and death: each creeps into the other very slowly and gradually. Every single minute death creeps into every living thing so as to be side by side with life. Death works into a living being and life builds up. Living cells die and disappear, while new living cells come into existence and begin their work. Those cells which have died come back to life in a different cycle, and what comes into life dies again in yet another cycle. All this happens within every single living thing. The circle, however, becomes wider and the living thing dies. Its cells, however, become minute particles that are incorporated in another formula, then enter the body of another living being and come back to life. It is an ever-continuing cycle that goes on throughout the day and night. No man claims to control or do any part of this whole process. No rational person can claim that it comes about by chance.

It is a complete cycle that goes on within the whole universe and every living thing. It is a fine, subtle and, at the same time, great cycle brought about before our own eyes and minds by this brief Qur'ānic statement. It is a strong pointer to the One Who can create, plan and control. How can human beings, then, try to isolate themselves and their affairs from the Creator Who controls and plans everything? How can they devise for themselves systems which satisfy their whims when they are only a sector of this universe, regulated by the Wise Who knows all? How can some of them enslave others? How can some look at others as gods when all of them look to God for their sustenance: **"You grant sustenance to whom You will, beyond all reckoning."**

This final touch puts our human hearts face to face with the greatest truism of the oneness of God: there is only one deity Who controls, sustains, plans, owns and grants sustenance to all. People must submit only to the Eternal Master of all, the Sovereign of all dominion, who exalts and abases, gives life and causes death, who gives His grace to whom He wills and withdraws it from whom He wills. In every situation, He ensures justice and brings about what is good.

(8) Surah al-A'raf (7: 54-56)

إِنَّ رَبَّكُمُ ٱللَّهُ ٱلَّذِى خَلَقَ ٱلسَّمَٰوَٰتِ وَٱلْأَرْضَ فِى سِتَّةِ أَيَّامٍ ثُمَّ ٱسْتَوَىٰ عَلَى ٱلْعَرْشِ يُغْشِى ٱلَّيْلَ ٱلنَّهَارَ يَطْلُبُهُۥ حَثِيثًا وَٱلشَّمْسَ وَٱلْقَمَرَ وَٱلنُّجُومَ مُسَخَّرَٰتٍ بِأَمْرِهِۦٓ أَلَا لَهُ ٱلْخَلْقُ وَٱلْأَمْرُ تَبَارَكَ ٱللَّهُ رَبُّ ٱلْعَٰلَمِينَ ﴿٥٤﴾ ٱدْعُواْ رَبَّكُمْ تَضَرُّعًا وَخُفْيَةً إِنَّهُۥ لَا يُحِبُّ ٱلْمُعْتَدِينَ ﴿٥٥﴾ وَلَا تُفْسِدُواْ فِى ٱلْأَرْضِ بَعْدَ إِصْلَٰحِهَا وَٱدْعُوهُ خَوْفًا وَطَمَعًا إِنَّ رَحْمَتَ ٱللَّهِ قَرِيبٌ مِّنَ ٱلْمُحْسِنِينَ ﴿٥٦﴾

7-54. Inna Rabbakkumul laahul lazee khalaqas sammaawaati
wal arda
fee sittati ayyaamin summmas tawaa 'alal 'arshi
yughshil lailan nahaara yatlu buhoo haseesanw washshamsa
walqamara wannujooma musakhkharaatim bi amrih;
alaa lahul khalqu wal-amr; tabaarakal laahu Rabbul
'aalameen.
7-55. Ud'oo Rabbakum tadarru'anw wa khufyah; innahoo laa
yuhibbul mu'tadeen.
7-56. Wa laa tufsidoo fil ardi ba'da islaahihaa wad'oohu
khawfanw wa tama'aa;
inna rahmatal laahi qareebum minal muhsineen.

Translation: *Your Guardian-Lord is Allah, who created the*
heavens and the earth in six days, and is firmly established on the
throne (of authority): He draweth the night as a veil o'er the day,
each seeking the other in rapid succession: He created the sun, the
moon, and the stars, (all) governed by laws under His command.
Is it not His to create and govern? Blessed be Allah, the Cherisher
and Sustainer of the worlds! (54) Call on your Lord with humility
and in private: for Allah loveth not those who trespass beyond
bounds. (55) Do no mischief on the earth, after it hath been set in
order, but call on Him with fear and longing (in your hearts): for
the Mercy of Allah is (always) near to those who do good.
(Surah al-A'raf, 7: 54-56)

(7:54) The monotheistic Islamic faith allows no room for any
attempt by human beings to work out by themselves any
particular concept of God: what He is like or how He acts. There
is simply nothing similar to God in any way whatsoever. Hence,
it is not up to the human intellect to try to picture the Supreme
Being. A human concept can only be worked out within the
framework that the human intellect can define, based on what it
makes out of the world around it. Since there is simply nothing
similar to God, then the human intellect cannot draw any
definite picture of what God is like. Moreover, it simply cannot

visualize how His actions take place. The only alternative available to man is to reflect on the effects of God's actions in the universe around him.

The Qur'ān uses the expression yawm, which means 'day', as it speaks of the period in which God created the heavens and the earth. Their creation was over six such yawm or six days. Again, this belongs to the realm that lies beyond the reach of human perception. Nothing of this creation has been witnessed by any human being or indeed by any creature: **"I did not call them to witness at the creation of the heavens and the earth, nor at their own creation."** (18: 51)

Whatever is said about these six days is not based on any certain knowledge. They may be six stages of creation or six epochs or six of God's days which cannot be measured by our time which is the result of the movement of certain planets and stars. Before these were created, time, as we know it, did not exist. Still, the six days to which the Qur'ānic verse refers may be something totally different. Hence, no one may claim that he has certain knowledge of what this figure truly means.

Any attempt to interpret this statement, and similar ones, based on human theories, and to justify that as being `scientific' is simply arbitrary. It betrays defeatism under the pressure of 'science' which can do no more in this area than the formulation of theories that cannot be proven.

God, who has created this vast and awesome universe and established His own high position, conducting the operation of the universe and administering its affairs, is the One who throws the veil of the night over the day in swift pursuit. Thus, the night follows the day in quick succession. It is He who has made the sun, the moon and the stars subservient to His will and He is the Creator and the controller of all. It is He, then, who is worthy of being "your Lord", giving you sustenance. He gives you the system which ensures your unity and the legislation which settles your disputes. To Him belongs all creation and all authority. Since He is the only Creator, He is also the only one who has any authority. It is this question of Godhead, Lordship and sovereignty, as well as the fact that all belong to God alone which constitute the theme of this passage, and indeed the whole sūrah. Its correlative is the question of submission by human beings to God and their implementation of His law in their lives.

(7: 55) Thus, the human consciousness is overawed by the lively scenes of the universe which is used to look at in a dull inattentive way. Coupled with this is the realization that all these great creatures submit to the authority of the Creator. At this point, the sūrah reminds human beings of their only Lord and directs them to call upon Him with humility and full submission. They must acknowledge His Lordship to keep within the limits of their submission to Him, recognizing His authority and refraining from creating or spreading corruption in the land by abandoning His law and following their capricious desires.

This directive is made at the most appropriate point, with human beings in the proper frame of mind. They are directed to call upon their Lord and address Him with humility and submission. They should also call on Him in the secrecy of their hearts, not making loud noises. A secret appeal to God is much more befitting because it affirms the close relationship between man and his Lord. Muslim, the renowned ĥadīth scholar, relates this authentic ĥadīth to the authority of Abū Mūsā who reports: "We were with God's Messenger on one of his travels — (in one version it is stated that this took place when they were on a military expedition) — and people started to glorify God out loud. God's Messenger said to them: "O you people, gently and quietly. You are not calling on someone who is deaf or absent. You are calling on the One who hears all and is close at hand. He is true with you."

The Qur'ānic drift stresses the consciousness that God, in His Majesty, is so close to man. This is described herein in its practical form as we make our supplication to God. A person who is conscious of God's majesty feels too modest to appeal to Him in a loud voice. If we realize that He is so close to us we can have no reason for appealing to Him loudly. Along with this scene of sincere supplication to God and complete humiliation before Him, an order is issued not to try to usurp His authority as the Arabs used to do in their days of ignorance, when they claimed sovereignty for themselves, while all sovereignty belongs to God alone.

(7: 56) They are further commanded not to spread corruption in the land by following their capricious desires after God has set the earth in proper order and laid down the law to govern both the earth and human life. A believing soul, which calls on its Lord with humility and in secrecy, feeling His closeness and ready response, is not given to aggression and corruption. The two attitudes are closely related in the depth of the human soul and feelings. In its approach, the Qur'ān touches on those feelings. It is an approach designed by the Creator who knows His creation and is fully aware of everything.

"Call on Him with fear and hope," (Verse 56), fearing to incur His anger and punishment, and hoping to earn His pleasure and reward. **"Truly, God's grace is ever near to the righteous,"** (Verse 56), who worship God as though they see Him. If they do not see him, they are fully aware that He sees them. This is the attitude defined by the Prophet as belonging to the righteous.

(9) Surah al-Isra' (17: 110-111)

قُلِ ٱدْعُواْ ٱللَّهَ أَوِ ٱدْعُواْ ٱلرَّحْمَٰنَ ۖ أَيًّا مَّا تَدْعُواْ فَلَهُ ٱلْأَسْمَآءُ ٱلْحُسْنَىٰ ۚ وَلَا تَجْهَرْ بِصَلَاتِكَ وَلَا تُخَافِتْ بِهَا وَٱبْتَغِ بَيْنَ ذَٰلِكَ سَبِيلًا ﴿١١٠﴾

وَقُلِ ٱلْحَمْدُ لِلَّهِ ٱلَّذِى لَمْ يَتَّخِذْ وَلَدًا وَلَمْ يَكُن لَّهُۥ شَرِيكٌ فِى ٱلْمُلْكِ وَلَمْ يَكُن لَّهُۥ وَلِىٌّ مِّنَ ٱلذُّلِّ ۖ وَكَبِّرْهُ تَكْبِيرًا ﴿١١١﴾

17-110. Qulid'ul laaha awid'ur Rahmaana ayyam maa tad'oo
falahul asmaaa'ul Husnaa;
wa laa tajhar bi Salaatika wa laa tukhaafit bihaa wabtaghi
baina zaalika sabeela.
17-111. Wa qulil hamdu lillaahil lazee lam yattakhiz
waladanw wa lam yakul lahoo shareekun fil mulki wa lam
yakul lahoo
waliyyum minaz zulli wa kabbirhu takbeeraa.

102

Translation: Say, "Call upon Allah, or call upon Rahman: by whatever name ye call upon Him, (it is well): for to Him belong the Most Beautiful Names. Neither speak thy Prayer aloud, nor speak it in a low tone, but seek a middle course between." (110) Say, "Praise be to Allah, who begets no son, and has no partner in (His) dominion: Nor (needs) He any to protect Him from humiliation: yea, magnify Him for His greatness and glory!" (111)

(Surah al-Isra', 17: 110-111)

This Surah is a wonderful balance of warning and instruction. The disbelievers of Makkah are warned to take a lesson from the chastisement of the Israelites and other past civilisations. They should therefore accept the message of Islam before they too are annihilated and replaced.

(17: 110) This inspiring scene is painted after the sūrah has given the Arabs the choice of believing in the Qur'ān or rejecting it. It is followed with a statement leaving it up to them to call on God with whatever names they choose. In their days of ignorance, they declined to call God Raĥmān, which means, 'Most Merciful'. Hence, they are told that they may call on God with whichever one of His names they choose:

"Say: Call upon God or call upon the Most Merciful. By whichever name you invoke Him, His are the most gracious names." (Verse 110)

Their prejudices concerning His names have no basis other than a myth that they used to believe in their ignorance. They have no sound basis.

The Prophet is then instructed to recite his prayers in a middle voice. This is because the unbelievers used to ridicule him whenever they saw him praying. It is also true to say that a voice pitched in the middle is the most suited to prayer:

"Do not raise your voice too loud in prayer, nor say it is too low a voice, but follow a middle course in between." (Verse 110)

(17: 111) The sūrah closes in the same way as it opened, praising God and asserting His oneness, and reiterating the facts that He has neither son nor partner and requires no help or support from anyone. This is indeed the pivot around which the sūrah turns:

"And say: All praise is due to God who has never begotten a son; who has no partner in His dominion; who needs none to support Him against any difficulty.' And extol His greatness." (Verse 111)

(10) Surah al-Mu'minun (23: 115-118)

أَفَحَسِبْتُمْ أَنَّمَا خَلَقْنَٰكُمْ عَبَثًا وَأَنَّكُمْ إِلَيْنَا لَا تُرْجَعُونَ ﴿١١٥﴾

فَتَعَٰلَى ٱللَّهُ ٱلْمَلِكُ ٱلْحَقُّ لَآ إِلَٰهَ إِلَّا هُوَ رَبُّ ٱلْعَرْشِ ٱلْكَرِيمِ ﴿١١٦﴾

وَمَن يَدْعُ مَعَ ٱللَّهِ إِلَٰهًا ءَاخَرَ لَا بُرْهَٰنَ لَهُۥ بِهِۦ فَإِنَّمَا حِسَابُهُۥ عِندَ رَبِّهِۦٓ إِنَّهُۥ لَا يُفْلِحُ ٱلْكَٰفِرُونَ ﴿١١٧﴾

وَقُل رَّبِّ ٱغْفِرْ وَٱرْحَمْ وَأَنتَ خَيْرُ ٱلرَّٰحِمِينَ ﴿١١٨﴾

23-115. Afahsibtum annamaa khalaqnaakum 'abasanw wa annakum ilainaa laa turja'oon
23-116. Fata'aalal laahul Malikul Haqq; laaa ilaaha illaa Huwa Rabbul 'Arshil Kareem.
23-117. Wa mai yad'u ma'allaahi ilaahan aakhara laa burhaana

lahoo bihee
fa innnamaa hisaabuhoo 'inda Rabbih; innahoo laa yuflihul
kaafiroon.
23-118. Wa qur Rabbigh fir warham wa Anta khairur raahimeen.

Translation: "Did ye then think that We had created you in jest and that ye would not be brought back to Us (for account)?" (115) Therefore, exalted be Allah, the King, the Reality: there is no god but He, the Lord of the Throne of Honour! (116) If anyone invokes, besides Allah, Any other god, he has no authority, therefore; and his reckoning will be only with his Lord! and verily the Unbelievers will fail to win through! (117) So, say: "O my Lord! grant Thou forgiveness and mercy for Thou art the Best of those who show mercy!" (118)

(Surah al-Mu'minun, 23: 115-118)

This Surah was revealed in Mecca. At a time when there was the peak of a famine in the region. The intense friction had begun between Prophet Muhammad and the disbelievers, though persecution had not yet begun.

In this Surah, people are invited to accept and follow the Prophet. This is the central theme of the Surah. It speaks about the character of true believers and assures that they will be successful people. It draws attention to various stages of human creation, and to many other universal signs. Then it takes some of the stories of other prophets and tells us that they also preached the same message.

Allah (ﷻ) begins the Surah by mentioning the traits of those who will be successful and ends the Surah by mentioning the reason why the disbelievers will not be successful. Surah al-Mu'minum [The Believers] takes its name after the first Ayah,

قَدْ أَفْلَحَ الْمُؤْمِنُونَ

"Certainly, will the believers have succeeded." (23:1)

وَمَن يَدْعُ مَعَ ٱللَّهِ إِلَٰهًا ءَاخَرَ لَا بُرْهَٰنَ لَهُۥ بِهِۦ فَإِنَّمَا حِسَابُهُۥ عِندَ رَبِّهِۦٓ إِنَّهُۥ لَا يُفْلِحُ ٱلْكَٰفِرُونَ ﴿١١٧﴾

"And whoever invokes besides Allah another deity for which he has no proof - then his account is only with his Lord. Indeed, the disbelievers will not succeed. " (23:117)

(23:115) Again they are strongly rebuked for denying the life to come. This is coupled with an outline of the purpose behind the resurrection. This purpose has been clearly stated ever since the first creation. Indeed, the purpose, or rather the wisdom behind resurrection is part of the wisdom behind creation. It is all well-measured and accurately designed. Resurrection is no more than a stage that brings the cycle of creation to its fullness. Only those who remain blind, unwilling to reflect on God's purpose which is clearly evident everywhere in the universe around us, will not see it.

(23:116) The final verses of the sūrah are dedicated to faith. They state its central tenet; namely, God's oneness. We have an announcement of the great loss suffered by those who associate partners with Him. This contrasts with the success declared at the beginning of the sūrah which is guaranteed to the believers. Coupled with this declaration is an instruction to turn to God, requesting His forgiveness and appealing for His mercy. He is certainly the most merciful of all those who are compassionate.

Coming as it does after a scene painting events taking place on the Day of Resurrection, and after a host of arguments, proofs and pointers outlined throughout the sūrah, the comment included in these final verses provides a logical conclusion to everything contained in the sūrah. This statement refutes all that the unbelievers say about God, declaring that He is the true Sovereign who controls the entire universe and that He is the only deity who is in full command of all. He is indeed 'the Lord of the Glorious Throne'.

(23:117) Any claim of partnership with God has no evidence to support it, neither from the universe and how it is run nor from human logic or nature. Anyone who makes such a claim will have to face the reckoning in front of God, and the result is known in advance: **"Most certainly the unbelievers shall never be successful."** This is an unfailing rule that is hound to come true. Success, by contrast, is guaranteed for the believers.

All the favours and comforts that we see the unbelievers enjoying in this life and all the power and resources they may sometimes have at their command do not mean success in reality. It is all given to them as a test, and it will end with their loss in this present life. However, if some of them escape punishment in this world, they will have to face the reckoning in the hereafter. There, in the life to come, is the final stage of this life cycle. It is not something separate or isolated. Indeed, it is an essential stage, clearly seen by those who have real vision.

(23:118) The last verse in this sūrah, The Believers, instructs us to turn to God appealing for His mercy and forgiveness. Thus, the opening of the sūrah and its end jointly emphasize success for the believers and utter failure and loss for the unbelievers. Both elements stress the basic qualities of believers. Thus, the beginning states that the believers humble themselves in prayer, while the end instructs them to humbly appeal to God for forgiveness and mercy. Both make the sūrah a complete, well-designed unit.

(11) Surah al-Saffat (37: 1-11)

بِسْمِ ٱللَّهِ ٱلرَّحْمَٰنِ ٱلرَّحِيمِ

وَٱلصَّٰٓفَّٰتِ صَفًّا ﴿١﴾ فَٱلزَّٰجِرَٰتِ زَجْرًا ﴿٢﴾ فَٱلتَّٰلِيَٰتِ ذِكْرًا ﴿٣﴾ إِنَّ إِلَٰهَكُمْ لَوَٰحِدٌ ﴿٤﴾ رَّبُّ ٱلسَّمَٰوَٰتِ وَٱلْأَرْضِ وَمَا بَيْنَهُمَا وَرَبُّ ٱلْمَشَٰرِقِ ﴿٥﴾ إِنَّا زَيَّنَّا ٱلسَّمَآءَ ٱلدُّنْيَا بِزِينَةٍ ٱلْكَوَاكِبِ ﴿٦﴾ وَحِفْظًا مِّن كُلِّ شَيْطَٰنٍ مَّارِدٍ ﴿٧﴾ لَّا يَسَّمَّعُونَ إِلَى ٱلْمَلَإِ ٱلْأَعْلَىٰ وَيُقْذَفُونَ مِن كُلِّ جَانِبٍ ﴿٨﴾ دُحُورًا وَلَهُمْ عَذَابٌ وَاصِبٌ ﴿٩﴾ إِلَّا مَنْ خَطِفَ ٱلْخَطْفَةَ فَأَتْبَعَهُ شِهَابٌ ثَاقِبٌ ﴿١٠﴾ فَٱسْتَفْتِهِمْ أَهُمْ أَشَدُّ خَلْقًا أَم مَّنْ خَلَقْنَا ۚ إِنَّا خَلَقْنَٰهُم مِّن طِينٍ لَّازِبٍ ﴿١١﴾

37-1. Wassaaaffaati saffaa
37-2. Fazzaajiraati zajraa
37-3. Fattaaliyaati Zikra
37-4. Inna Illaahakum la Waahid
37-5. Rabbus samaawaati wal ardi wa maa bainahumaa wa
Rabbul mashaariq
37-6. Innaa zaiyannas samaaa 'ad dunyaa bizeenatinil kawaakib
37-7. Wa hifzam min kulli Shaitaanim maarid
37-8. Laa yassamma 'oona ilal mala il a'alaa wa yuqzafoona min
kulli jaanib
37-9. Duhooranw wa lahum 'azaabunw waasib
37-10. Illaa man khatifal khatfata fa atba'ahoo shihaabun saaqib
37-11. Fastaftihim ahum ashaddu khalqan am man khalaqnaa;
innaa khalaqnaahum min teenil laazib.

Translation: *By those [angels] lined up in rows(1) And those
who drive [the clouds](2) And those who recite the message,(3)
Indeed, your God is One,(4) Lord of the heavens and the earth and
that between them and Lord of the sunrises.(5) Indeed, We have
adorned the nearest heaven with an adornment of stars(6) And as
protection against every rebellious devil(7) [So] they may not
listen to the exalted assembly [of angels] and are pelted from
every side,(8) Repelled; and for them is a constant punishment,(9)
Except one who snatches [some words] by theft, but they are
pursued by a burning flame, piercing [in brightness]. (10) Then
inquire of them, [O Muhammad], "Are they a stronger [or more
difficult] creation or those [others] We have created?" Indeed, we
created men from sticky clay. (11)*

(Surah al-Saffat, 37: 1-11)

The Surah speaks about the oneness of Allah (ﷻ) in very

strong terms. It talks about the teachings of various prophets of

Allah (ﷻ). All of them preached the same message. It gives warnings to the non-believers that their plots against the message of Islam will not work. The truth will prevail.

Surah as-Saffat takes its name from the first Ayat,

وَالصَّافَّاتِ صَفًّا

(37:1) "By those [angels] lined up in rows"

The sūrah begins by mentioning three groups of people, and identifying what they do. The first description may mean that they range themselves in rows as they pray, or range their wings, awaiting God's commands.

(37:2) "And those who drive [the clouds] ..."

The second group rebukes whoever deserves rebuke, perhaps at the time when the angels gather their souls when they die, or at the time of resurrection, or when they are driven into hell, or in any position or situation.

(37:3) "And those who recite the message,"

The third group recite God's word, which may be the Qur'ān or other scriptures or they may recite glorifications of God.

(37:4) The three groups are mentioned in the form of an oath made by God confirming His oneness: "**Your God is One.**" (Verse 4) As we have already stated, the occasion here is the mention of the superstition circulated in ignorant Arabia alleging that the angels were God's daughters, and as such, they too were deities.

(37:5) God then mentions to His servants something about Himself that is suited to the truth of His oneness: He is the "**Lord of the heavens and the earth and everything between them, Lord of all the points of sunrise.**" (Verse 5) The heavens and the earth stand before us, speaking to us about the Creator who controls everything in this universe. No one else claims the ability to create and control the universe, and no one can deny that the One who created the universe is the true Lord who has absolute power. He also created and controls "**everything between them**," including the air, clouds, light, as well as tiny little creatures which man comes to know from time to time, but much more remains unknown to man. It is impossible to look with an alert mind at the heavens and the earth and what is between them without being profoundly affected by the greatness, accuracy, variety, beauty, harmony and coherence between all these creatures. Only a dead heart can look at them without genuine interaction.

"Lord of all points of sunrise."

The translation of this verse is far from adequate, as the verse not only refers to the rising of the sun but of every star and planet. Each has its time and point of rising. Therefore, the number of such points in all the corners of the universe is beyond imagination. At the same time, the phrase refers to the fact that as the earth turns around the sun, every point of it has its own sunrise and its point of sunset. Whenever a point of the earth is facing the sun, it has its sunrise, and the opposite point on the surface of the earth has its sunset. People did not know this at the time of the revelation of the Qur'ān, but God told them about it. This precise system that makes such successive sunrises over the earth and the splendid beauty that so permeates our planet beckons us to reflect on the superb beauty of God's creation and to believe in His oneness. How could such beauty, accuracy and consistency have been achieved unless the Maker is One?

(37:6) At the outset, the sūrah touches on the part of the superstition that relates to angels. Now it touches on the part that relates to the jinn. In pre-Islamic days, some Arabs alleged that the jinn was related to God. Indeed, some of them worshipped the jinn for this reason, and because they attributed it to their knowledge of the world beyond human perception.

"Indeed, we have adorned the nearest heaven with an adornment of stars"

One look at the sky is sufficient to realize that the element of beauty is purposely incorporated into the making of the universe: its very make-up is beautiful, well-proportioned and harmonious. Beauty is an essential part of its nature. Its design gives equal importance to its beautiful appearance and perfect functioning. Therefore, everything in it is made according to an accurate measure, performing its role to perfection and adding to its overall beauty.

(37:7-9) Another function of the stars and their satellites is also mentioned in the sūrah, demonstrating how some of them are shooting stars and piercing flames that target the jinn, preventing them from getting close to those on high.

This means that some of the shooting stars we see guard the skies against rebellious devils to prevent them from eavesdropping on those on high. Such devils on the Day of Judgement will be punished further. However, a rebellious devil might stealthily snatch something of what goes on among the angels on high, but as this devil descends, a piercing flame pursues and burns him.

(37:10) We have no idea how the rebellious devil tries to eavesdrop, how he snatches a fragment, or how he is pursued by the piercing flame. All of these are beyond the limits of our human nature and the power of imagination. The only way open to us is to believe what we are told by God and accept it as it is stated. We should remember that our knowledge of the universe is only superficial. What is important to understand here is that those devils who are prevented from eavesdropping on what takes place on high are the ones whom the idolaters alleged to be related to God. Had anything of the sort been true, the whole story would have been totally different. Such alleged relatives would not have suffered the burning fate that pursues them.

(37:11) Receiving the Message with Ridicule

The Prophet is then instructed to question them about whether they considered their creation to be more difficult or the creation of the heavens, earth and all creation in the universe? If they agree that man's creation is less difficult, why should they then disbelieve in the resurrection, meeting it with derision and considering it impossible, when it is nothing compared to creating the universe?

The other created beings in this respect include the angels, heavens, the earth and all between them, the jinn, stars, planets and piercing flames. They acknowledge that these are created by God. No answer, however, is expected to the question. This is simply a rhetorical device inviting amazement at their lack of understanding of what is around them. It derides the way they look at things. Leaving the question unanswered, the sūrah shows them the substance from which they were created in the first place: it is soft, sticky clay made of material from this earth, which is itself one of God's creatures: "They have We created out of a sticky clay." (Verse 11) It is abundantly clear then that they are not the more difficult to create. Hence, their making fun of God's signs and His promise to bring them back to life is nothing less than absurd.

(12) Surah al-Rahman (55: 33-40)

يَٰمَعْشَرَ ٱلْجِنِّ وَٱلْإِنسِ إِنِ ٱسْتَطَعْتُمْ أَن تَنفُذُوا۟ مِنْ أَقْطَارِ ٱلسَّمَٰوَٰتِ وَٱلْأَرْضِ فَٱنفُذُوا۟ لَا تَنفُذُونَ إِلَّا بِسُلْطَٰنٍ ﴿٣٣﴾ فَبِأَىِّ ءَالَآءِ رَبِّكُمَا تُكَذِّبَانِ ﴿٣٤﴾ يُرْسَلُ عَلَيْكُمَا شُوَاظٌ مِّن نَّارٍ وَنُحَاسٌ فَلَا تَنتَصِرَانِ ﴿٣٥﴾ فَبِأَىِّ ءَالَآءِ رَبِّكُمَا تُكَذِّبَانِ ﴿٣٦﴾ فَإِذَا ٱنشَقَّتِ ٱلسَّمَآءُ فَكَانَتْ وَرْدَةً كَٱلدِّهَانِ ﴿٣٧﴾ فَبِأَىِّ ءَالَآءِ رَبِّكُمَا تُكَذِّبَانِ ﴿٣٨﴾ فَيَوْمَئِذٍ لَّا يُسْـَٔلُ عَن ذَنۢبِهِۦٓ إِنسٌ وَلَا جَآنٌّ ﴿٣٩﴾ فَبِأَىِّ ءَالَآءِ رَبِّكُمَا تُكَذِّبَانِ ﴿٤٠﴾

55-33. Yaa ma'sharal jinni wal insi inis tata'tum an tanfuzoo
min aqtaaris samaawaati wal ardi fanfuzoo;
laa tanfuzoona illaa bisultaan.
55-34. Fabi ayyi aalaaa'i Rabbikumaa tukazzibaan.
55-35. Yursalu 'alaikumaa shuwaazum min naarifiw-wa nuhaasun
falaa tantasiraan
55-36 Fabi ayyi aalaaa'i Rabbikumaa tukazzibaan.
55-37 Fa-izan shaqqatis samaaa'u fakaanat wardatan kaddihaan
55-38 Fabi ayyi aalaaa'i Rabbikumaa tukazzibaan.
55-39 Fa-yawma'izil laa yus'alu 'an zambiheee insunw wa laa
jaann
55-40 Fabi ayyi aalaaa'i Rabbikumaa tukazzibaan.

Translation: O company of jinn and mankind, if you are able
to pass beyond the regions of the heavens and the earth, then
pass. You will not pass except by authority [from Allah]. (33) So,
which of the favours of your Lord would you deny? (34) There
will be sent upon you a flame of fire and smoke, and you will not
defend yourselves. (35) So, which of the favours of your Lord
would you deny? (36) And when the heaven is split open and
becomes rose-coloured like oil -(37) So which of the favours of
your Lord would you deny? -(38) Then on that Day, none will be
asked about his sin among men or jinn. (39) So, which of the
favours of your Lord would you deny? (40)

(Surah al-Rahman, 55: 33-40)

The Surah indicates that Prophet Muhammad is Allah's
Prophet and Messenger for both human beings as well as
Jinns. Allah's many blessings and favours are mentioned in this
Surah. Human beings and Jinn are invited to remember these
favours and not to deny Allah's blessings. This Surah takes its

name after the name of Allah (ﷻ)mentioned in the first Ayat,

116

"The Most Merciful" (55:1).   This is the **only** Surah of the Qur'an that begins with the name of Allah, in this case, ar-Rahman.

Owing to the sura's poetic beauty, it is often regarded as the 'beauty of the Quran', in accordance with a hadith: Abdullah ibn Mas'ud reported that Muhammad said, "Everything has an adornment, and the adornment of the Qur'an is Surah ar Rahman"

(55:33) The surah continues with this frightening tone, challenging both man and jinn to pass beyond their own world: **"Jinn and mankind if you can pass beyond the regions of heaven and earth, then do so." (Verse 33)** How, and where to? **"You cannot pass beyond them without authority." (Verse 33)** No authority can be given except by the One who has it.

(55:34) No authority can be given except by the One who has it. Once more, they are faced with the question: **"Which, then, of your Lord's blessings do you both deny?"**

(55:35-36) A flash of fire will be sent against you, and molten brass, and you will be left without support. Which, then, of your Lord's blessings do you both deny?

(55:37) The surah devotes its remaining part to images and scenes of the Last Day, starting with a universal upheaval, followed by images of reckoning, requital and reward. This commences with an image of the universe that fits with the opening of the surah: **"When the sky is rent asunder and becomes rose-red like [burning] oil." (Verse 37)** We are introduced to a picture of the sky turning rose-red or looking like a red rose and flowing like oil. The sum of the verses describing the universe on the Day of Judgement confirms the total destruction of all celestial bodies after they break loose of the system which controls their operation and coordinates their orbits and movements. One of these verses is the one we are now discussing.

(55:38) **"When the sky is rent asunder and becomes rose-red like [burning] oil." (Verse 37)** The same question is again asked: **"Which, then, of your Lord's blessings do you both deny?" (Verse 38)** No denial can then be either contemplated or uttered.

(55:39) **"On that day neither mankind nor jinn will be asked about their sins."** This applies to a particular situation on that day when all will be present. It is a day with different situations: in some people will be questioned and, in others, no question will be put to them. In some, every soul will argue its case, trying to blame its associates, and in others, no word of argument or dispute will be allowed. It is a long, extended day, with many positions and situations, each of which is awesome, and each is witnessed by multitudes of creatures. This verse speaks of a particular situation when no human or jinn will be asked about their sins. Everything is already well known, and the deeds of all are out in the open. Signs of misery appear as black on some faces, and signs of triumph appear white on others. Every face tells of what is going to happen. Can there be any denial on that day?

(55:40) This verse speaks of a particular situation when no human or jinn will be asked about their sins. Everything is already well known, and the deeds of all are out in the open. Signs of misery appear as black on some faces, and signs of triumph appear white on others. Every face tells of what is going to happen. Can there be any denial on that day?

Hence, the question: **"Which, then, of your Lord's blessings do you both deny?"**

(13) Surah al-Hashar (59: 21-24)

لَوْ أَنزَلْنَا هَٰذَا ٱلْقُرْءَانَ عَلَىٰ جَبَلٍ لَّرَأَيْتَهُ خَٰشِعًا مُّتَصَدِّعًا مِّنْ خَشْيَةِ ٱللَّهِ ۚ وَتِلْكَ ٱلْأَمْثَٰلُ نَضْرِبُهَا لِلنَّاسِ لَعَلَّهُمْ يَتَفَكَّرُونَ ۞ ٢١ ۞ هُوَ ٱللَّهُ ٱلَّذِى لَآ إِلَٰهَ إِلَّا هُوَ ۖ عَٰلِمُ ٱلْغَيْبِ وَٱلشَّهَٰدَةِ ۖ هُوَ ٱلرَّحْمَٰنُ ٱلرَّحِيمُ ۞ ٢٢ ۞ هُوَ ٱللَّهُ ٱلَّذِى لَآ إِلَٰهَ إِلَّا هُوَ ٱلْمَلِكُ ٱلْقُدُّوسُ ٱلسَّلَٰمُ ٱلْمُؤْمِنُ ٱلْمُهَيْمِنُ ٱلْعَزِيزُ ٱلْجَبَّارُ ٱلْمُتَكَبِّرُ ۚ سُبْحَٰنَ ٱللَّهِ عَمَّا يُشْرِكُونَ ۞ ٢٣ ۞ هُوَ ٱللَّهُ ٱلْخَٰلِقُ ٱلْبَارِئُ ٱلْمُصَوِّرُ ۖ لَهُ ٱلْأَسْمَآءُ ٱلْحُسْنَىٰ ۚ يُسَبِّحُ لَهُ مَا فِى ٱلسَّمَٰوَٰتِ وَٱلْأَرْضِ ۖ وَهُوَ ٱلْعَزِيزُ ٱلْحَكِيمُ ۞ ٢٤ ۞

*59-21. Law anzalnaa haazal quraana 'alaa jabilil lara aytahoo
khaashi'am muta saddi
'am min khashiyatil laah; wa tilkal amsaalu nadribuhaa
linnaasi la'allahum yatafakkaroon.*
*59-22. Huwal-laahul-lazee laaa Ilaaha illaa Huwa 'Aalimul
Ghaibi wash-shahaada; Huwar Rahmaanur-Raheem.*
*59-23. Huwal-laahul-lazee laaa Ilaaha illaa Huwal-Malikul
Quddoosus-Salaamul Muminul Muhaiminul-'aAzeezul
Jabbaarul-Mutakabbir;
Subhaanal laahi 'Ammaa yushrikoon.*
*59-24. Huwal Laahul Khaaliqul Baari 'ul Musawwir; lahul
Asmaaa'ul Husnaa;
yusabbihu lahoo maa fis samaawaati wal ardi wa Huwal
'Azeezul Hakeem.*

Translation: *Had We sent down this Qur'an on a mountain,
verily, thou wouldst have seen it humble itself and cleave asunder
for fear of Allah. Such is the similitude which We propound to
men, that they may reflect. (21) Allah is He, than Whom there is
no other god; - Who knows (all things) both secret and open; He,
Most Gracious, Most Merciful. (22) Allah is He, than Whom there
is no other god; - the Sovereign, the Holy One, the Source of Peace
(and Perfection), the Guardian of Faith, the Preserver of Safety,
the Exalted in Might, the Irresistible, the Supreme: Glory to Allah!
(High is He) above the partners they attribute to Him. (23) He is
Allah, the Creator, the Evolve-er, the Bestow-er of Forms (or
Colours). To Him belong the Most Beautiful Names: whatever is in
the heavens and on earth, doth declare His Praises and Glory: and
He is the Exalted in Might, the Wise. (24)*

(Surah al-Hashar, 59: 21-24)

Narrated Ma'qil bin Yasar:

that the Prophet (ﷺ) said: "Whoever says three times when he gets up in the morning: 'A'udhu Billahis-Sami Al-'Alim Min Ash-Shaitanir-Rajim' and he recites three Ayat from the end of Surah Al-Hashr - Allah appoints seventy-thousand angels who say Salat upon him until the evening. If he dies on that day, he dies a martyr, and whoever reaches the evening, he holds the same status."

حَدَّثَنَا مَحْمُودُ بْنُ غَيْلاَنَ، قَالَ حَدَّثَنَا أَبُو أَحْمَدَ الزُّبَيْرِيُّ قَالَ حَدَّثَنَا خَالِدُ بْنُ طَهْمَانَ أَبُو الْعَلاَءِ الْخَفَّافُ، قَالَ حَدَّثَنِي نَافِعُ بْنُ أَبِي نَافِعٍ، عَنْ مَعْقِلِ بْنِ يَسَارٍ، عَنِ النَّبِيِّ صلى الله عليه وسلم قَالَ " مَنْ قَالَ حِينَ يُصْبِحُ ثَلاَثَ مَرَّاتٍ أَعُوذُ بِاللَّهِ السَّمِيعِ الْعَلِيمِ مِنَ الشَّيْطَانِ الرَّجِيمِ وَقَرَأَ ثَلاَثَ آيَاتٍ مِنْ آخِرِ سُورَةِ الْحَشْرِ وَكَّلَ اللَّهُ بِهِ سَبْعِينَ أَلْفَ مَلَكٍ يُصَلُّونَ عَلَيْهِ حَتَّى يُمْسِيَ وَإِنْ مَاتَ فِي ذَلِكَ الْيَوْمِ مَاتَ شَهِيدًا وَمَنْ قَالَهَا حِينَ يُمْسِي كَانَ بِتِلْكَ الْمَنْزِلَةِ " . قَالَ أَبُو عِيسَى هَذَا حَدِيثٌ غَرِيبٌ لاَ نَعْرِفُهُ إِلاَّ مِنْ هَذَا الْوَجْهِ .

Grade: Da'if (Darussalam)

Reference: Jami` at-Tirmidhi 2922

In-book Reference: Book 45, Hadith 48
English **Translation**: Vol. 5, Book 42, Hadith 2922

The Surah talks about the banishment of Bani Nadhir and secret relations between them and the hypocrites of Madinah. It exhorts the Believers to be firm in their faith in Allah and gives some of the Beautiful Names of Allah. The power of Allah in aiding and assisting the Believers.

The Surah takes its name from the second Ayat,

هُوَ الَّذِي أَخْرَجَ الَّذِينَ كَفَرُوا مِنْ أَهْلِ الْكِتَابِ مِن دِيَارِهِمْ
لِأَوَّلِ الْحَشْرِ

"It is He who expelled the ones who disbelieved among the People of the Scripture from their homes at the first gathering...." [59:2]

(59:21) It portrays what effect the Qur'an would have had on solid rocks had it been so sent down. This image reflects the truth. This Qur'an has such weight, power and shaking influence that is irresistible when we receive it as it truly is. `Umar ibn al-Khattab had such an experience when he overheard a reciter reading the opening of *Surah* 52: **"By Mount Sinai; by a scripture inscribed on unrolled parchment; by the much-visited House; by the vault raised high; by the swelling sea; your Lord's punishment will indeed come to pass. Nothing can stop it..." (52: 1-8)** As he listened, he leaned on a wall nearby. He then went back home and felt ill. People kept visiting him for a month, enquiring about his health.

Ibn Kathir wrote on the ayat: "God the Exalted emphasizes the greatness of the Qur'an, its high status and of being worthy of making hearts humble and rent asunder upon hearing it, because of the true promises and sure threats that it contains."

The moments when a person is fully receptive to some truth contained in the Qur'an will see him shake and shudder. He will experience such changes that are best represented in the physical world by the effects of magnetism and electricity or even stronger. God, the Creator of the mountains who bestowed the Qur'an from on high, says: **"If We had sent down this Qur'an upon a mountain, you would have seen it humbled and coming apart from fear of Allah."** Anyone who has had some experience of the Qur'an touching their inner souls will appreciate this truth in a way that cannot be otherwise expressed. Such an image should keep hearts thinking and reflecting.

Narrated 'Atiyyah: from Abu Sa'eed, that the Messenger of Allah (ﷺ) said: "The Lord, Blessed and Most High is He, has said: 'Whoever is too busy with the Qur'an for remembering Me and asking Me, then I shall give him more than what I give to those who ask.' And the virtue of Allah's Speech over the speech of others is like the virtue of Allah over His creation.

حَدَّثَنَا مُحَمَّدُ بْنُ إِسْمَاعِيلَ، قَالَ حَدَّثَنَا شِهَابُ بْنُ عَبَّادٍ الْعَبْدِيُّ، قَالَ حَدَّثَنَا مُحَمَّدُ بْنُ الْحَسَنِ بْنِ أَبِي يَزِيدَ الْهَمْدَانِيُّ، عَنْ عَمْرِو بْنِ قَيْسٍ، عَنْ عَطِيَّةَ، عَنْ أَبِي سَعِيدٍ، قَالَ قَالَ رَسُولُ اللَّهِ صلى الله عليه وسلم " يَقُولُ الرَّبُّ عَزَّ وَجَلَّ مَنْ شَغَلَهُ الْقُرْآنُ عَنْ ذِكْرِي وَ مَسْأَلَتِي

أَعْطَيْتُهُ أَفْضَلَ مَا أُعْطِي السَّائِلِينَ وَفَضْلُ كَلَامِ اللَّهِ عَلَى سَائِرِ الْكَلَامِ كَفَضْلِ اللَّهِ عَلَى خَلْقِهِ " . هَذَا حَدِيثٌ حَسَنٌ غَرِيبٌ .

Grade: Da'if (Darussalam)

Reference: Jami` at-Tirmidhi 2926
In-book Reference: Book 45, Hadith 52
English **Translation:** Vol. 5, Book 42, Hadith 2926

(59:22) The rest of the *surah* is devoted to a long glorification of God, citing a number of His names and attributes. This serves as an aspect of the influence of the Qur'an on the universe. It is as if we see the universe as a person expressing this glorification with his mouth, and a vast kingdom echoing it in every corner. These attributes of God have clear effects on the very nature of the universe, its phenomena and interactions. As it offers this glorification, it testifies to the truth of these attributes and their effects.

"He is Allah, other than whom there is no deity, "These imprints on our consciousness the truth of God's oneness in belief, worship, action and life conduct from the beginning of creation to its end. Based on this oneness, a whole code of living is based, on regulating our way of thinking, feeling, behaviour, relations with the universe and its living creatures, as well as relations with people.

"Knower of the unseen and the witnessed." This divine attribute makes us conscious of God's knowledge of everything, apparent or hidden. This awakes in our consciences the need to watch out, keeping God always in our thoughts, public and private. Thus, man will go about his life feeling that he is being watched by God and that he is on the watch for God's sake, realizing that he does not live alone, not even when he is in seclusion or locked alone with one other in private conversation. His actions will be coloured by this feeling that keeps him always on guard.

"He is the Entirely Merciful, the Especially Merciful." Now a feeling of reassurance spreads within man's conscience as he feels the air of God's mercy spread over him. Feelings of awe and hope, *fear* and reassurance are well balanced within him. In the believer's concept, God does not chase His creatures, but watches them; He does not wish them harm, but loves that they should adhere to His guidance; He does not abandon them to struggle against evil without providing help for them.

Al-Hafiz Ibn Kathir wrote: "God states that He Alone is worthy of worship, there is no Lord or God for the existence, except Him. All that are being worshipped instead of God are false deities. God is the All-Knower in the unseen and the seen, He knows all that pertains to the creations that we see, and those we cannot see. Nothing in heaven or on earth ever escapes His knowledge, no matter how great or insignificant, big or small, including ants in darkness. "God's statement, 'He is the Most Gracious, the Most Merciful... asserts that God is the Owner of the wide encompassing mercy that entails all of His creation. He is Ar-Rahman and Ar-Rahim of this life and the Hereafter."

(59:23) "He is Allah, other than whom there is no deity" This is repeated at the beginning of the second part of this expansive glorification of God because it provides the basis for all divine attributes.

"The Sovereign." This attribute imprints on our hearts the truth that there is no sovereignty or dominion to anyone other than God who has no partners. When there is one sovereign, those who are subject to that sovereignty will have only one master to serve. No one can serve two masters at the same time:

"The Pure" This attribute radiates absolute holiness and purity It strikes our hearts with purity, keeps them cleansed, suited to receive the grace of the Holy Sovereign, and all to extol His limitless glory.

"The bestow-er of Faith." The very pronunciation of this attribute, *al-MuMin,* gives a believer a clear sense of the value of faith. Here, a believer meets with God and draws on one of His attributes, rising by virtue of his faith to join the community on high.

"The overseer." This begins a new set of attributes that contribute to our concept of Him. The previous attributes related to Him only. These new ones relate to His action as He conducts life, the universe and all affairs. These attributes imply His absolute control and watchfulness.

The same applies to the other three attributes stated in this verse, "**The Exalted in Might, the Compeller, the Superior.**" They all emphasize power, authority and superiority. None is more powerful or has greater authority than Him, just as no one can be in any way superior to Him. These attributes belong to God alone; none share them with Him in any way. Hence the verse ends with the statement: **"Exalted is Allah above whatever they associate with Him."**

Al-Hafiz Ibn Kathir then set out the meaning of God's Names that are listed in Ayah 23. He wrote that Al-Malik means "The Owner and King of all things, who has full power over them without resistance or hindrance". He explained that Al-Quddus, means "'The Pure', according to Wahb bin Munabbih, while Mujahid and Qatadah said that Al-Quddus means 'The Blessed'.

Ibn Jurayj said that Al-Quddus means 'He whom the honourable angels glorify'." As-Salam, means "Free from any defects or shortcomings that lessen or decrease His perfect attributes and actions" while Al-Mu'min means one "Who has granted safety to His servants by promising that He will never be unjust to them. According to Ad-Dahhak who reported it from Abd Allah ibn Abbas. Qatadah said that Al-Mu'min means that 'God affirms that His statements are true, while Ibn Zayd said that it means, 'He attested to His faithful servants' having faith in Him. Al-Hafiz Ibn Kathir noted that Al-Muhaymin meant, according to Ibn 'Abbas and others, 'The Witness for His servant's actions, that is the Ever-Watcher over them.

Al-Aziz means "He is the Almighty, Dominant over all things. Therefore, His majesty is never violated, due to His might, greatness, irresistible power and pride". Al-Jabbar, Al-Mutakabbir means "The Only One worthy of being the Compeller and Supreme. There is a Hadith in the Sahih Collection in which God said: 'Might is my Izar and pride is My Rida; if anyone disputes any one of them with Me, then I will punish him.'"

(59:24) The last verse of the *surah* begins the third section of this expansive glorification of God, and again it begins with a statement of His oneness: **"He is Allah."** He is **"the Creator, the inventor."** The Creator stresses design and proportion, while the Maker stresses the process of bringing things into reality, The two attributes are intertwined, and the difference between them is subtle. **"The Fashioner"** This attribute is also closely related to the two before it. It means that God is the One who gives every creature its distinctive features and specific qualities that make up its personality.

The succession of these interlinked qualities, with their subtle differences, prompts us to follow the process of creation and initiation, stage by stage, as we humans conceive of it. There are no stages or steps. What we know of these attributes is not their absolute reality, because this is known only to God. We only know some of the effects they produce, as this is the limit of our understanding.

"To Him belong the best names" His names are, in themselves, most gracious. They need not be praised or admired by creatures. The Arabic adjective *al-husnd,* translated here as *'the most gracious',* also means 'beautiful, attractive, etc.' They are the attributes a believer reflects upon to mould himself and his life by their meaning. He knows that God loves that he should try to live up to them so that he can elevate himself as He seeks God's acceptance.

This long and expansive glorification of God, citing many of His most gracious attributes, with all their inspiring effects, is brought to a close with the image that God's glorification is echoed throughout the universe, with every creature joining in: **"Whatever is in the heavens and earth is exalting Him. And He is the Exalted in Might, the Wise."** These are the most suitable and expected images after the mention of all God's attributes. Thus, the human heart joins in with all creatures and living things in a glorification that brings the opening of the surah and its ending into perfect harmony.

Commenting on Ayah 24, Ibn Kathir wrote: "Al-Khaliq refers to measuring and proportioning, Al-Bari refers to inventing and bringing into existence What he has created and measured. Surely, none except God can measure, bring forth and create whatever He wills to come to existence. God's statement, Al-Khaliq, Al-Bari, Al-Musawwir means, if God wills something, He merely says to it 'be' and it comes to existence in the form that He wills and the shape He chooses."

(14) Surah al-Jinn (72: 1-4)

بِسْمِ ٱللَّهِ ٱلرَّحْمَٰنِ ٱلرَّحِيمِ

قُلْ أُوحِىَ إِلَىَّ أَنَّهُ ٱسْتَمَعَ نَفَرٌ مِّنَ ٱلْجِنِّ فَقَالُوٓاْ إِنَّا سَمِعْنَا قُرْءَانًا عَجَبًا ۝ ١ يَهْدِىٓ إِلَى ٱلرُّشْدِ فَـَٔامَنَّا بِهِۦ وَلَن نُّشْرِكَ بِرَبِّنَآ أَحَدًا ۝ ٢ وَأَنَّهُۥ تَعَٰلَىٰ جَدُّ رَبِّنَا مَا ٱتَّخَذَ صَٰحِبَةً وَلَا وَلَدًا ۝ ٣ وَأَنَّهُۥ كَانَ يَقُولُ سَفِيهُنَا عَلَى ٱللَّهِ شَطَطًا ۝ ٤

72-1. *Qul oohiya ilaiya annna hustama'a nafarum minal jinnni faqaalooo innaa sami'naa quraanan 'ajabaa.*

72-2 *Yahdeee ilar rushdi fa aamannaa bihee wa lan nushrika bi rabbinaaa ahadaa.*

72-3 *Wa annahoo Ta'aalaa jaddu Rabbinaa mat takhaza saahibatanw wa la waladaa.*

72-4 *Wa annahoo kaana yaqoolu safeehunaa 'alal laahi shatataa.*

Translation: *Say, [O Muhammad], "It has been revealed to me that a group of the jinn listened and said, 'Indeed, we have heard an amazing Qur'an. (1) It guides us to the right course, and we have believed in it. And we will never associate with our Lord anyone. (2) And [it teaches] that exalted is the nobleness of our Lord; He has not taken a wife or a son (3) And that our foolish one has been saying about Allah an excessive transgression. (4)*

(Surah al-Jinn, 72: 1-4)

The Surah gives assurance that the message of Allah (ﷺ)

will be accepted. It talks about some Jinn (a hidden creation) who accepted the message and, in this way, gives a prediction that if the present people deny the message, then others, yet hidden, will accept this message.

`Urwah said:

I heard 'lkrimah (recite): "And (remember) when We sent

towards you (Muhammad (ﷺ))" and it was recited to Sufyan

from az-Zubair, `a group (three to ten persons) of the jinn, (quietly) listening to the Qur`an` (al-Ahqaf [46:29]). He said:

"[That was] in Nakhlah. The Messenger of Allah (ﷺ) was

praying Isha`, and they (the jinn) just made round him a dense crowd as if sticking one over the other (to listen to the Prophet's

(ﷺ) recitation)" (al-Jinn [72:19]). Sufyan said: "They were one

above the other, like thick masses of clouds one above the other."

حَدَّثَنَا سُفْيَانُ، قَالَ عَمْرُو وَسَمِعْتُ عِكْرِمَةَ، {وَإِذْ صَرَفْنَا إِلَيْكَ}

وَقُرِئَ عَلَى سُفْيَانَ عَنِ الزُّبَيْرِ نَفَرًا مِنَ الْجِنِّ يَسْتَمِعُونَ الْقُرْآنَ قَالَ

بِنَخْلَةَ وَرَسُولُ اللَّهِ صَلَّى اللَّهُ عَلَيْهِ وَسَلَّمَ يُصَلِّي الْعِشَاءَ الْآخِرَةَ كَادُوا

يَكُونُونَ عَلَيْهِ لِبَدًا قَالَ سُفْيَانُ كَانَ بَعْضُهُمْ عَلَى بَعْضٍ كَاللَّبَدِ بَعْضُهُ

عَلَى بَعْضٍ.

Grade: Hasan because of corroborating evidence and Da'if (Darussalam) because it is interrupted between Ikrimah and Az-Zubair] (Darussalam)

Reference: Musnad Ahmad 1435

In-book Reference: Book 7, Hadith 28

In this Surah in v. 1-15, we are informed about the impact of the Qur'an on the company of the Jinn; when they heard it and what they said to their fellow Jinn when they returned to them. God, in this connection, has not cited their whole conversation but only those particular things which were worthy of mention. That is why the style is not that of a continuous speech but sentences have been cited to indicate that they said this and that. If one studies these sentences spoken by the Jinn carefully, one can easily understand the reason for the narration of this event; their affirming the faith and mentioning their conversation with their people in the Qur'an.

(72:1) The first thing they realise about the Qur'anic discourse is that it is unfamiliar and that it makes the listener wonder. This is how the Qur'an is received by anyone who listens with an open and positive mind. He will find that the Qur'an contains intrinsic power, strong appeal and beautiful music that touch hearts and feelings. It is 'wondrous' indeed, which tells us that the group.

(72:2) It is true that the Qur'an guides to what is right and sensible, but the term 'sagacious' also connotes maturity and wisdom that distinguishes right from wrong. It adds an element of awareness that naturally guides to the truth and to what is right and good. It establishes a bond with the source of light and guidance, as well as harmony with major universal laws. In doing so, the Qur'an guides to what is sagacious, as indeed it does by providing a code of living the like of which has never been experienced by any other human community. Yet this system enabled individuals and communities to attain sublime standards in personal morality and values as well as in social relations.

This is the natural and sound reaction to listening to the Qur'an and understanding its nature. The verse puts this response to the unbelievers in Makkah who used to listen to the Qur'an but who would not believe in it. They even attributed it to the jinn, alleging that the Prophet was a soothsayer, a poet or a madman, influenced by the jinn. Here, we see the jinn wondering at the Qur'an, profoundly influenced by its discourse, unable to resist it. We see them able to discern the truth and submit to it. They could not turn away from the truth they felt.

Theirs, then, is a case of complete faith, untainted by delusions, superstitions or any element of polytheism. It is faith-based on understanding the truth presented by the Qur'an, i.e., the truth of God's absolute oneness.

(72:3) The verses use the Arabic word jadd, attributing it to God. This word connotes share, position, authority and greatness. All these connotations are meant here. Hence the translation of the first sentence in the verse. What is intended here is to impart a clear feeling of God's greatness and His being far above taking a wife or child for Himself. The Arabs used to allege that the angels were God's daughters through marriage to the jinn. Now the jinn denies such a superstition most expressively. They glorify God and deny that such a notion could ever have happened. The jinn would have proudly proclaimed such a connection had there been any possibility of it ever having taken place. Their denial delivers a massive blow at the unbelievers' baseless claims, and indeed at every similar claim alleging that God has taken a son to Himself in any way, shape or form.

(72:4) This is a critical examination of what the jinn used to hear some of the foolish among them say. Those are the ones who did not believe in God's oneness and who alleged that He had a wife, a son and partners. Now that they have heard the Qur'an, they realize this is all false. Those who promote such ideas are, therefore, foolish, lacking a sound mind. They explain their own earlier belief of what those foolish ones said by the fact that they could not imagine that any creature, human or jinn, would ever perpetrate a lie about God. To them, that was an absolute enormity. Therefore, when those foolish people told them that God had a wife, a son and partners, they believed them because they could not conceive of how anyone would knowingly utter an untruth about God.

(15) Surah al-Kafirun (109: 1-6)

بِسْمِ اللَّهِ الرَّحْمَٰنِ الرَّحِيمِ

قُلْ يَٰٓأَيُّهَا ٱلْكَٰفِرُونَ ۝١ لَآ أَعْبُدُ مَا تَعْبُدُونَ ۝٢

وَلَآ أَنتُمْ عَٰبِدُونَ مَآ أَعْبُدُ ۝٣ وَلَآ أَنَا۠ عَابِدٌ مَّا عَبَدتُّمْ

۝٤ وَلَآ أَنتُمْ عَٰبِدُونَ مَآ أَعْبُدُ ۝٥ لَكُمْ دِينُكُمْ وَلِىَ

دِينِ ۝٦

Bismillaahir Rahmaanir Raheem.

109-1. Qul yaa-ai yuhal kaafiroon
109-2. Laa a'budu ma t'abudoon
109-3. Wa laa antum 'aabidoona maa a'bud
109-4. Wa laa ana 'abidum maa 'abattum
109-5. Wa laa antum 'aabidoona ma a'bud
109-6. Lakum deenukum wa liya deen.

Translation: *In the name of Allah, Most Gracious, Most Merciful. Say, "O disbelievers, (1) I do not worship what you worship. (2) Nor are you worshippers of what I worship. (3) Nor will I be a worshipper of what you worship. (4) Nor will you be worshippers of what I worship. (5) For you is your religion, and for me is my religion."(6)*

(Surah al-Kafirun, 109: 1-6)

The Surah tells us that there cannot be any compromise in matters of faith and worship. People are free to follow whatever religion they want, but the truth and falsehood cannot be mixed.

Like many of the shorter surahs, the surah of the unbelievers takes the form of an invocation, telling the reader something they must ask for or say aloud. Here, the passage asks one to keep in mind the separation between belief and unbelief both in the past and the present, ending with the often-cited line "To you your religion, and to me mine". Although some view this as an argument against religious intolerance, others see it as a more time-specific revelation, warning the newly founded Muslim minority in Mecca against being induced (by the Quraysh Arab tribe majority) to collude with disbelievers.

It was revealed in Mecca when the Muslims were persecuted by the polytheists of Mecca.

Both Fardah bin Naufal and Abdur Rahman bin Naufal have stated that their father, Naufal bin Muawiyah al-Ashjai, said to Muhammad: "Teach me something which I may recite at the time I go to bed." Muhammad replied: "Recite قُلْ يَٰٓأَيُّهَا ٱلْكَٰفِرُونَ to the end and then sleep, for this is immunity from polytheism." A similar request was made by Jabalah bin Harithah, brother of Said bin Harithah, to Muhammad and to him also he gave the same reply.

(109:1) Following one form of negation, assertion and emphasis after another, the surah sets its message in absolute clarity. It starts with the word, 'Say,' which denotes a clear divine order stressing the fact that the whole affair of religion belongs exclusively to God. Nothing of it belongs to Muhammad himself. Moreover, it implies that God is the only one to order and decide. Address them, Muhammad, by their actual identity. They follow no prescribed religion, nor do they believe in you. No meeting point exists between you and them anywhere. Thus, the beginning of the surah brings to mind the reality of difference which cannot be ignored or overlooked.

(109:2) When Muhammad (peace be upon him) declared his religion to be that of Abraham, they argued that there was no reason for them to forsake their beliefs and follow Muhammad's instead since they too were of the same religion. In the meantime, they sought a sort of compromise with him proposing that he should prostrate himself before their deities in return for their prostration to his God and that he should cease denouncing their deities and their manner of worship in reciprocation for whatever he demanded of them! This confusion in their concepts, vividly illustrated by their worship of various deities while acknowledging God, was perhaps what led them to believe that the gulf between them and Muhammad was not unbridgeable. They thought an agreement was somehow possible by allowing the two camps to co-exist in the region and by granting him some personal concessions!

To clear up this muddle, to cut all arguments short and to firmly distinguish between one form of worship and the other, and indeed between one faith and the other, this surah was revealed in such a decisive, assertive tone. It was revealed in this manner to demarcate monotheism, i.e., tawhid, from polytheism, i.e. shirk, and to establish a true criterion, allowing no further wrangling or vain argument.

(109:3) They follow no prescribed religion, nor do they believe in you. No meeting point exists between you and them anywhere.

(109:4-5) This is repeated for added emphasis and to eliminate all doubt or misinterpretation.

(109:6) Finally, the whole argument is summed up in the last verse. This means that you, unbelievers, and I, Muhammad, are very far apart, without any bridge to connect us. This is a complete distinction and a precise, intelligible demarcation.

Such an attitude was essential to expose the fundamental discrepancies in the essence, source and concepts of the two beliefs, i.e., between monotheism and polytheism, faith and unbelief. Faith is the way of life that directs man and the whole world towards God alone and determines for him the source of his religion, laws, values, criteria, ethics and morality. That source is God. Thus, life proceeds for the believer, devoid of any form of idolatry. Idolatry on the other hand is the opposite of faith. The two never meet.

Jahiliyyah and Islam are two different entities, separated by a wide gulf. The only way to bridge that gulf is for jahiliyyah to liquidate itself completely and substitute for all its laws, values, standards and concepts for their Islamic counterparts. The first step that should be taken in this respect by the person calling on people to embrace Islam is to segregate himself from jahiliyyah. He must be separated to the extent that any agreement or intercourse between him and jahiliyyah is impossible unless and until the people of jahiliyyah embrace Islam completely: no intermingling, no half measures or conciliation is permissible, however clever jahiliyyah may be in usurping or reflecting the role of Islam. The chief characteristic of a person who calls on others to adopt Islam is the clarity of this fact within himself and his solemn conviction of being radically different from those who do not share his outlook. They have their own religion, and he has his. His task is to change their standing point so that they may follow his path without false pretence or compromise. Failing this, he must withdraw completely, detach himself from their life and openly declare to them.

Without this basic separation confusion, double-dealing, doubt and distortion will certainly persist. And let it be clear in our minds here that the movement advocating Islam can never be constructed on any ambiguous or feeble foundations, but has to be built upon firmness, explicitness, frankness and fortitude as embodied in God's instruction to us to declare.

(16) Surah al-Ikhlas (112: 1-4)

بِسْمِ ٱللَّهِ ٱلرَّحْمَٰنِ ٱلرَّحِيمِ

قُلْ هُوَ ٱللَّهُ أَحَدٌ ﴿١﴾ ٱللَّهُ ٱلصَّمَدُ ﴿٢﴾ لَمْ يَلِدْ وَلَمْ يُولَدْ ﴿٣﴾ وَلَمْ يَكُن لَّهُ كُفُوًا أَحَدٌ ﴿٤﴾

Bismillaahir Rahmaanir Raheem.

112-1. Qul huwal laahu ahad
112-2. Allah hus-samad
112-3. Lam yalid wa lam yoolad
112-4. Wa lam yakul-lahu kufuwan ahad

Translation: *In the name of Allah, Most Gracious, Most Merciful. Say: He is Allah, the One and Only; (1) Allah, the Eternal, Absolute; (2) He begotten not, nor is He begotten; (3) And there is none like unto Him. (4)*

(Surah al-Ikhlas, 112: 1-4)

This is a great Surah of Tawhid. It speaks about the oneness of Allah. The Surah is named al-Ikhlas - which can be translated as 'pure, complete, sincerity'. Interestingly, the word does not appear in the Surah itself.

Reciting Surah Al Ikhlas is believed to be the means of earning Allah's love and attaining paradise. It also banishes poverty and increases sustenance. In addition, the constant recitation of this Surah makes a person worthy of having the archangel Jibreel participate in his/her funeral prayer. It is said to be equal in value to a third part of the whole Quran.

Narrated Abu Said Al-Khudri:

A man heard another man reciting (Surah-Al-Ikhlas) 'Say He is Allah, (the) One.' (112. 1) repeatedly. The next morning, he came to Allah's Messenger (ﷺ) and informed him about it as if he thought that it was not enough to recite. On that Allah's Messenger (ﷺ) said, "By Him in Whose Hand my life is, this Surah is equal to one-third of the Qur'an!"

حَدَّثَنَا عَبْدُ اللَّهِ بْنُ يُوسُفَ، أَخْبَرَنَا مَالِكٌ، عَنْ عَبْدِ الرَّحْمَنِ بْنِ

عَبْدِ اللَّهِ بْنِ عَبْدِ الرَّحْمَنِ بْنِ أَبِي صَعْصَعَةَ، عَنْ أَبِيهِ، عَنْ أَبِي سَعِيدٍ

الْخُدْرِيِّ، أَنَّ رَجُلاً، سَمِعَ رَجُلاً، يَقْرَأُ }قُلْ هُوَ اللهُ أَحَدٌ{ يُرَدِّدُهَا فَلَمَّا

أَصْبَحَ جَاءَ إِلَى رَسُولِ اللَّهِ صلى الله عليه وسلم فَذَكَرَ ذَلِكَ لَهُ وَكَأَنَّ الرَّجُلَ يَتَقَالُّهَا فَقَالَ رَسُولُ اللَّهِ صلى الله عليه وسلم " وَالَّذِي نَفْسِي بِيَدِهِ إِنَّهَا لَتَعْدِلُ ثُلُثَ الْقُرْآنِ ".

Reference: Sahih al-Bukhari 5013
In-book Reference: Book 66, Hadith 35
USC-MSA web (English) Reference: Vol. 6, Book 61, Hadith 533

It is mentioned in Musnad of Ahmad, Sunan of Tirmidhi and others that a group of Mushrikeen or Yahud came to the Prophet (peace be upon him) and asked, "Describe to us your Lord" or "Mention your Lord's lineage to us". So this Surah was revealed.

(112:1) This surah firmly establishes and confirms the Islamic belief in God's oneness. The Unbelievers is a denunciation of any similarity or meeting point between the Islamic concept of God's oneness and any belief that ascribes human form, attributes, or personality to God.

Ahad - This name of Allah means 'uniquely one' - and amazingly only occurs once in the Qur'an as Allah's Name - whereas his many other Names are mentioned numerous times.

(112:2) This means the Lord to whom all creation turns for help, and without whose permission, nothing is decided. God is the One and only Lord. He is the One God and Master while all other beings are but His servants. To Him and Him alone are addressed all prayers and supplications. He and only He decides everything independently. No one shares His authority.

In view of Ibn Abbas: **Samad** is he to whom the people turn when afflicted with a calamity. Still another view of his: The chieftain who in his chieftaincy, in his nobility and glory, in his clemency and forbearance, in his knowledge and wisdom is perfect.

(112:3) This means that the reality of God is deep-rooted, permanent and everlasting. No changeable circumstances ever affect it. Its quality is absolute perfection at all times. Birth is descent and multiplication and implies a developed being after incompleteness or nothingness. It requires espousal which is based on similarity of being and structure. All this is utterly impossible in God's case. So the quality of 'One' includes the renouncement of a father and a son.

(112:4) This means that no one resembles Him in anything or is equivalent to Him in any respect, either in their reality of being, in the fact that He is the only effective power, or in any of His qualities or attributes. This is implied in the statement of his being 'One' made in the first verse, but it is repeated to confirm and elaborate upon that fact. It is a renunciation of the two-God belief which implies that God is the God of Good while Evil has its own lord who, as the belief goes — is in opposition to God, spoils His good deeds and propagates evil on earth. The most well-known two-God belief was that of the Persians, who believed in a god of light and a god of darkness. This belief was known to the people in the south of the Arabian Peninsula, where the Persians once had a state and exercised sovereignty.

(17) Surah al-Falaq (113: 1-5)

بِسْمِ ٱللَّهِ ٱلرَّحْمَٰنِ ٱلرَّحِيمِ

قُلْ أَعُوذُ بِرَبِّ ٱلْفَلَقِ ﴿١﴾ مِن شَرِّ مَا خَلَقَ ﴿٢﴾ وَمِن شَرِّ غَاسِقٍ إِذَا وَقَبَ ﴿٣﴾ وَمِن شَرِّ ٱلنَّفَّٰثَٰتِ فِى ٱلْعُقَدِ ﴿٤﴾ وَمِن شَرِّ حَاسِدٍ إِذَا حَسَدَ ﴿٥﴾

Bismillaahir Rahmaanir Raheem.

113-1. Qul a'uzoo bi rabbil-falaq
113-2. Min sharri ma khalaq
113-3. Wa min sharri ghasiqin iza waqab
113-4. Wa min sharrin-naffaa-saati fil 'uqad
113-5. Wa min shar ri haasidin iza hasad.

Translation: In the name of Allah, Most Gracious, Most Merciful. Say, "I seek refuge with the Lord of the Dawn (1) From the mischief of created things; (2) From the mischief of Darkness as it overspreads; (3) From the mischief of those who practise secret arts; (4) And from the mischief of the envious one as he practises envy. (5)

(Surah al-Falaq, 113: 1-5)

The Surah remind us that evil is lurching everywhere and things can become harmful. One should always be conscious, do the right things and seek Allah's protection.

This Surah takes its name from the first Ayat, قُلْ أَعُوذُ بِرَبِّ

الْفَلَقِ "Say, "I seek refuge in the Lord of daybreak" [113:1].

Uqbah bin Amir Al-Juhni narrated that:

the Prophet said: "Allah has revealed to me Ayat the likes of which have not been seen: "Say: I seek refuge in the Lord of mankind..." until the end of the Surat. "Say: I seek refuge in the Lord of Al-Falaq..." until the end of the Surat.

حَدَّثَنَا مُحَمَّدُ بْنُ بَشَّارٍ، حَدَّثَنَا يَحْيَى بْنُ سَعِيدٍ، عَنْ إِسْمَاعِيلَ بْنِ

أَبِي خَالِدٍ، حَدَّثَنِي قَيْسٌ، وَهُوَ ابْنُ أَبِي حَازِمٍ عَنْ عُقْبَةَ بْنِ عَامِرٍ الْجُهَنِيِّ

عَنِ النَّبِيِّ صلى الله عليه وسلم قَالَ " قَدْ أَنْزَلَ اللَّهُ عَلَىَّ آيَاتٍ لَمْ يُرَ

مِثْلُهُنَّ :) قل أَعُوذُ بِرَبِّ النَّاسِ (إِلَى آخِرِ السُّورَةِ وَ :)قل أَعُوذُ بِرَبِّ

الْفَلَقِ (إِلَى آخِرِ السُّورَةِ " . قَالَ أَبُو عِيسَى هَذَا حَدِيثٌ حَسَنٌ صَحِيحٌ .

Grade: Sahih (Darussalam)

Reference: Jami` at-Tirmidhi 3367
In-book Reference: Book 47, Hadith 419
English **Translation:** Vol. 5, Book 44, Hadith 3367

(113:1) God — limitless is He in His glory — refers to Himself in this surah as the Lord of the daybreak. The Arabic term, falaq, simply means 'daybreak', but it could be taken to mean 'the whole phenomenon of creation,' with Reference to everything springing forth into life. If the meaning 'daybreak' is adopted, refuge is being sought from the unseen and the mysterious with the Lord of the daybreak, who bestows safety as He kindles the light of day.

(113:2) The phrase contains no exceptions or specifications. Mutual contact between various creatures, though no doubt advantageous, brings about some evil. Refuge from it is sought with God by the believers to encourage the goodness such contact produces. For He who created those creatures is surely able to provide the right circumstances that lead them on a course where only the bright side of their contact prevails.

(113:3) What is probably meant here is the night, with all that accompanies it when it rapidly engulfs the world. This is terrifying in itself. In addition, it fills our hearts with the possibility of an unknown, unexpected discomfort caused by a savage beast, an unscrupulous villain, a striking enemy or a hissing poisonous creature, as well as anxieties and worries [which may lead to depression and uneasiness], evil thoughts and passions that are liable to revive in the dark, during one's state of solitude at night. This is the evil against which the believer needs God's protection.

(113:4) This verse refers to various types of magic, whether by deceiving people's physical senses or by influencing their willpower and projecting ideas onto their emotions and minds. The verse especially refers to a form of witchcraft carried out by women in Arabia at the time who tied knots in cords and blew upon them with an imprecation.

Magic is the production of illusions, subject to a magician's designs, and it does not offer any kind of new facts or alter the nature of things. This is how the Qur'an describes magic when relating the story of Moses in Surah 20, Taha.

(113:5) Envy is the evil, begrudging reaction one feels towards another who has received some favour from God. It is also accompanied by a very strong desire for the end to such favours. It is also possible that some harm to the envied may result from such a baseless grudge. This may either be the outcome of direct physical action by the envier or from suppressed feelings alone.

We should not be uneasy to learn that there are countless inexplicable mysteries in life. There are several phenomena for which no account has been offered up till now. Telepathy and hypnosis are two such examples.

We should not try to deny the psychological effects of envy on the envied person just because we cannot ascertain how this takes place by scientific means and methods. Very little is known about the mysteries of envy and the little that is known has often been uncovered by chance and coincidence. In any case, there is in envy an evil from which the refuge and protection of God must be sought. For He, the Most Generous, Most Merciful, who knows all things, has directed the Prophet and his followers to seek His refuge from such evil. It is unanimously agreed by all Islamic schools of thought that God will always protect His servants from such evils, should they seek His protection as He has directed them to do.

(18) Surah al-Nas (114: 1-6)

سْمِ ٱللَّهِ ٱلرَّحْمَٰنِ ٱلرَّحِيمِ

قُلْ أَعُوذُ بِرَبِّ ٱلنَّاسِ ﴿١﴾ مَلِكِ ٱلنَّاسِ ﴿٢﴾ إِلَٰهِ ٱلنَّاسِ ﴿٣﴾ مِن شَرِّ ٱلْوَسْوَاسِ ٱلْخَنَّاسِ ﴿٤﴾ ٱلَّذِى يُوَسْوِسُ فِى صُدُورِ ٱلنَّاسِ ﴿٥﴾ مِنَ ٱلْجِنَّةِ وَٱلنَّاسِ ﴿٦﴾

Bismillaahir Rahmaanir Raheem.

114-1. Qul a'uzu birabbin naas
114-2. Malikin naas
114-3. Ilaahin naas
114-4. Min sharril was waasil khannaas
114-5. Al lazee yuwas wisu fee sudoorin naas
114-6. Minal jinnati wan naas.

Translation: *In the name of Allah, Most Gracious, Most Merciful. Say: I seek refuge with the Lord and Cherisher of Mankind, (1) The King (or Ruler) of Mankind, (2) The god (or judge) of Mankind, - (3) From the mischief of the Whisperer (of Evil), who withdraws (after his whisper),- (4) (The same) who whispers into the hearts of Mankind, (5) Among Jinns and among men. (6)*

(Surah Al-Nas, 114: 1-6)

The Surah tells us that Satan is always against human beings and he puts wrong suggestions in their minds. We should seek Allah's protection from Satan and his whisperings. This is a very appropriate ending for the Book of Allah (ﷻ). The Book of God is to protect from all evil and success under the guidance of Allah (ﷻ).

(114:2) For the Lord is He who preserves, directs, cherishes and protects mankind; the Sovereign is He who owns, governs and independently runs the world; and God is the One who supersedes all other beings and supervises over all their affairs. The particular mention of mankind here brings man closer to God's protection and care.

(114:3) God is the One who supersedes all other beings and supervises over all their affairs. The particular mention of mankind here brings man closer to God's protection and care

(114:4) We do not know how the jinn performs this whispering, but we certainly find its repercussions in the behaviour of individuals as well as in human life generally. We know for sure that the battle between Adam (man) and Iblis (Satan) is a very old one. The war between the two was declared by Satan out of the evil inherent in him, his conceit, envy and resentment of man. He was given God's permission to carry out this battle for some purpose that only God knows. But, significantly, man has not been left alone, dispossessed of the necessary means of protection. He has been provided with the power of faith, [that is, conscious belief in, and knowledge of, God and His attributes through conviction and sincere devotion]. Meditation and seeking refuge in God are among the most effective weapons.

If Satan ever excites you to anger, seek refuge with Allah (ﷻ). Say,

$$ \text{وَقُل رَّبِّ أَعُوذُ بِكَ مِنْ هَمَزَٰتِ ٱلشَّيَٰطِينِ ﴿٩٧﴾} $$

(23:97) And pray: "My Lord! I seek Your refuge from the suggestions of the evil ones;

(114:5) The style adopted here is quite significant because it draws our attention fully to the identity of this sneaking whisperer after describing its nature to show the process by which such evil is insinuated. This enables us to be alert and able to confront it. When we are given the full picture, we know that this sneaking whisperer operates secretly. We also realise that it can be either jinn or human, for human beings can easily spread their evil stealthily.

According to some scholars, these words mean that the whisperer whispers evil into the hearts of two kinds of people: the jinn and the men. The Quran says:

$$\text{وَكَذَٰلِكَ جَعَلْنَا لِكُلِّ نَبِيٍّ عَدُوًّا شَيَاطِينَ ٱلْإِنسِ وَٱلْجِنِّ يُوحِى بَعْضُهُمْ إِلَىٰ بَعْضٍ زُخْرُفَ ٱلْقَوْلِ غُرُورًا ۚ وَلَوْ شَاءَ رَبُّكَ مَا فَعَلُوهُ ۖ فَذَرْهُمْ وَمَا يَفْتَرُونَ ﴿١١٢﴾}$$

(6:112) And so it is that against every Prophet We have set up the evil ones from among men and jinn, some of them inspire others with specious speech only by way of delusion. Had it been your Lord's will, they would not have done it. Leave them alone to fabricate what they will.

And in the Hadith, lmam Ahmad, Nasai, and Ibn Hibban have related on the authority of Abu Dharr a tradition, saying: I sat before the Prophet (peace be upon him, who was in the Mosque. He said: Abu Dharr, have you performed the Prayer? I replied in the negative. He said: Arise and perform the Prayer. So, I performed the Prayer. The Prophet (peace be upon him) said: O Abu Dharr, seek Allah's refuge from the devils of men and the devils of jinn. I asked, are there devils among men also? O Messenger of Allah! He replied: Yes.

MANZIL COMPLETE

(1) Surah al-Fatihah (1: 1-7)

بِسْمِ ٱللَّهِ ٱلرَّحْمَٰنِ ٱلرَّحِيمِ ﴿١﴾

ٱلْحَمْدُ لِلَّهِ رَبِّ ٱلْعَٰلَمِينَ ﴿٢﴾

ٱلرَّحْمَٰنِ ٱلرَّحِيمِ ﴿٣﴾

مَٰلِكِ يَوْمِ ٱلدِّينِ ﴿٤﴾

إِيَّاكَ نَعْبُدُ وَإِيَّاكَ نَسْتَعِينُ ﴿٥﴾

ٱهْدِنَا ٱلصِّرَٰطَ ٱلْمُسْتَقِيمَ ﴿٦﴾

صِرَٰطَ ٱلَّذِينَ أَنْعَمْتَ عَلَيْهِمْ غَيْرِ ٱلْمَغْضُوبِ عَلَيْهِمْ

وَلَا ٱلضَّآلِّينَ ﴿٧﴾

(2) Surah al-Baqarah (2: 1-5)

بِسْمِ ٱللَّهِ ٱلرَّحْمَٰنِ ٱلرَّحِيمِ

الٓمٓ ﴿١﴾

ذَٰلِكَ ٱلْكِتَٰبُ لَا رَيْبَ ۛ فِيهِ ۛ هُدًى لِّلْمُتَّقِينَ ﴿٢﴾

ٱلَّذِينَ يُؤْمِنُونَ بِٱلْغَيْبِ وَيُقِيمُونَ ٱلصَّلَوٰةَ وَمِمَّا رَزَقْنَٰهُمْ

يُنفِقُونَ ﴿٣﴾

وَٱلَّذِينَ يُؤْمِنُونَ بِمَا أُنزِلَ إِلَيْكَ وَمَا أُنزِلَ مِن قَبْلِكَ

وَبِٱلْءَاخِرَةِ هُمْ يُوقِنُونَ ﴿٤﴾

أُو۟لَٰئِكَ عَلَىٰ هُدًى مِّن رَّبِّهِمْ ۖ وَأُو۟لَٰئِكَ هُمُ ٱلْمُفْلِحُونَ ﴿٥﴾

(3) Surah al-Baqarah (2: 163)

وَإِلَٰهُكُمْ إِلَٰهٌ وَٰحِدٌ ۖ لَّآ إِلَٰهَ إِلَّا هُوَ ٱلرَّحْمَٰنُ ٱلرَّحِيمُ ﴿١٦٣﴾

(4) Surah al-Baqarah (2: 255-257)

اللَّهُ لَا إِلَهَ إِلَّا هُوَ ٱلْحَىُّ ٱلْقَيُّومُ ۚ لَا تَأْخُذُهُ سِنَةٌ وَلَا نَوْمٌ ۚ لَّهُ مَا

فِى ٱلسَّمَوَتِ وَمَا فِى ٱلْأَرْضِ ۗ مَن ذَا ٱلَّذِى يَشْفَعُ عِندَهُۥ إِلَّا

بِإِذْنِهِۦ ۚ يَعْلَمُ مَا بَيْنَ أَيْدِيهِمْ وَمَا خَلْفَهُمْ ۖ وَلَا يُحِيطُونَ بِشَىْءٍ

مِّنْ عِلْمِهِۦ إِلَّا بِمَا شَآءَ ۚ وَسِعَ كُرْسِيُّهُ ٱلسَّمَوَتِ وَٱلْأَرْضَ ۖ وَلَا

يَُودُهُۥ حِفْظُهُمَا ۚ وَهُوَ ٱلْعَلِىُّ ٱلْعَظِيمُ ﴿٢٥٥﴾

لَا إِكْرَاهَ فِى ٱلدِّينِ ۖ قَد تَّبَيَّنَ ٱلرُّشْدُ مِنَ ٱلْغَىِّ ۚ فَمَن يَكْفُرْ

بِٱلطَّغُوتِ وَيُؤْمِن بِٱللَّهِ فَقَدِ ٱسْتَمْسَكَ بِٱلْعُرْوَةِ ٱلْوُثْقَىٰ لَا

ٱنفِصَامَ لَهَا ۗ وَٱللَّهُ سَمِيعٌ عَلِيمٌ ﴿٢٥٦﴾

ٱللَّهُ وَلِىُّ ٱلَّذِينَ ءَامَنُوا۟ يُخْرِجُهُم مِّنَ ٱلظُّلُمَتِ إِلَى ٱلنُّورِ ۖ

وَٱلَّذِينَ كَفَرُوٓا۟ أَوْلِيَآؤُهُمُ ٱلطَّغُوتُ يُخْرِجُونَهُم مِّنَ ٱلنُّورِ إِلَى

ٱلظُّلُمَتِ ۗ أُو۟لَٰئِكَ أَصْحَبُ ٱلنَّارِ ۖ هُمْ فِيهَا خَلِدُونَ ﴿٢٥٧﴾

(5) Surah al-Baqarah (2: 284-286)

لِّلَّهِ مَا فِى ٱلسَّمَٰوَٰتِ وَمَا فِى ٱلْأَرْضِ ۗ وَإِن تُبْدُوا۟ مَا فِىٓ أَنفُسِكُمْ أَوْ تُخْفُوهُ يُحَاسِبْكُم بِهِ ٱللَّهُ ۖ فَيَغْفِرُ لِمَن يَشَآءُ وَيُعَذِّبُ مَن يَشَآءُ ۗ وَٱللَّهُ عَلَىٰ كُلِّ شَىْءٍ قَدِيرٌ ﴿٢٨٤﴾

ءَامَنَ ٱلرَّسُولُ بِمَآ أُنزِلَ إِلَيْهِ مِن رَّبِّهِۦ وَٱلْمُؤْمِنُونَ ۚ كُلٌّ ءَامَنَ بِٱللَّهِ وَمَلَٰٓئِكَتِهِۦ وَكُتُبِهِۦ وَرُسُلِهِۦ لَا نُفَرِّقُ بَيْنَ أَحَدٍ مِّن رُّسُلِهِۦ ۚ وَقَالُوا۟ سَمِعْنَا وَأَطَعْنَا ۖ غُفْرَانَكَ رَبَّنَا وَإِلَيْكَ ٱلْمَصِيرُ ﴿٢٨٥﴾

لَا يُكَلِّفُ ٱللَّهُ نَفْسًا إِلَّا وُسْعَهَا ۚ لَهَا مَا كَسَبَتْ وَعَلَيْهَا مَا ٱكْتَسَبَتْ ۗ رَبَّنَا لَا تُؤَاخِذْنَآ إِن نَّسِينَآ أَوْ أَخْطَأْنَا ۚ رَبَّنَا وَلَا تَحْمِلْ عَلَيْنَآ إِصْرًا كَمَا حَمَلْتَهُۥ عَلَى ٱلَّذِينَ مِن قَبْلِنَا ۚ رَبَّنَا وَلَا تُحَمِّلْنَا مَا لَا طَاقَةَ لَنَا بِهِۦ ۖ وَٱعْفُ عَنَّا وَٱغْفِرْ لَنَا وَٱرْحَمْنَآ ۚ أَنتَ مَوْلَٰنَا فَٱنصُرْنَا عَلَى ٱلْقَوْمِ ٱلْكَٰفِرِينَ ﴿٢٨٦﴾

(6) Surah Aali Imran (3: 18)

شَهِدَ ٱللَّهُ أَنَّهُۥ لَآ إِلَٰهَ إِلَّا هُوَ وَٱلْمَلَٰئِكَةُ وَأُو۟لُوا۟ ٱلْعِلْمِ قَآئِمًۢا بِٱلْقِسْطِ ۚ لَآ إِلَٰهَ إِلَّا هُوَ ٱلْعَزِيزُ ٱلْحَكِيمُ ﴿١٨﴾

(7) Surah Aali Imran (3: 26-27)

قُلِ ٱللَّهُمَّ مَٰلِكَ ٱلْمُلْكِ تُؤْتِى ٱلْمُلْكَ مَن تَشَآءُ وَتَنزِعُ ٱلْمُلْكَ مِمَّن تَشَآءُ وَتُعِزُّ مَن تَشَآءُ وَتُذِلُّ مَن تَشَآءُ ۖ بِيَدِكَ ٱلْخَيْرُ ۖ إِنَّكَ عَلَىٰ كُلِّ شَىْءٍ قَدِيرٌ ﴿٢٦﴾ تُولِجُ ٱلَّيْلَ فِى ٱلنَّهَارِ وَتُولِجُ ٱلنَّهَارَ فِى ٱلَّيْلِ ۖ وَتُخْرِجُ ٱلْحَىَّ مِنَ ٱلْمَيِّتِ وَتُخْرِجُ ٱلْمَيِّتَ مِنَ ٱلْحَىِّ ۖ وَتَرْزُقُ مَن تَشَآءُ بِغَيْرِ حِسَابٍ ﴿٢٧﴾

(8) Surah al-A'raf (7: 54-56)

إِنَّ رَبَّكُمُ ٱللَّهُ ٱلَّذِى خَلَقَ ٱلسَّمَٰوَٰتِ وَٱلْأَرْضَ فِى سِتَّةِ أَيَّامٍ ثُمَّ ٱسْتَوَىٰ عَلَى ٱلْعَرْشِ يُغْشِى ٱلَّيْلَ ٱلنَّهَارَ يَطْلُبُهُ حَثِيثًا وَٱلشَّمْسَ وَٱلْقَمَرَ وَٱلنُّجُومَ مُسَخَّرَٰتٍ بِأَمْرِهِ أَلَا لَهُ ٱلْخَلْقُ وَٱلْأَمْرُ تَبَارَكَ ٱللَّهُ رَبُّ ٱلْعَٰلَمِينَ ﴿٥٤﴾

ٱدْعُوا۟ رَبَّكُمْ تَضَرُّعًا وَخُفْيَةً إِنَّهُۥ لَا يُحِبُّ ٱلْمُعْتَدِينَ ﴿٥٥﴾

وَلَا تُفْسِدُوا۟ فِى ٱلْأَرْضِ بَعْدَ إِصْلَٰحِهَا وَٱدْعُوهُ خَوْفًا وَطَمَعًا إِنَّ رَحْمَتَ ٱللَّهِ قَرِيبٌ مِّنَ ٱلْمُحْسِنِينَ ﴿٥٦﴾

(9) Surah al-Isra' (17: 110-111)

قُلِ ٱدْعُواْ ٱللَّهَ أَوِ ٱدْعُواْ ٱلرَّحْمَـٰنَ ۖ أَيًّا مَّا تَدْعُواْ فَلَهُ ٱلْأَسْمَآءُ ٱلْحُسْنَىٰ ۚ وَلَا تَجْهَرْ بِصَلَاتِكَ وَلَا تُخَافِتْ بِهَا وَٱبْتَغِ بَيْنَ ذَٰلِكَ سَبِيلًا ﴿١١٠﴾

وَقُلِ ٱلْحَمْدُ لِلَّهِ ٱلَّذِى لَمْ يَتَّخِذْ وَلَدًا وَلَمْ يَكُن لَّهُ شَرِيكٌ فِى ٱلْمُلْكِ وَلَمْ يَكُن لَّهُ وَلِىٌّ مِّنَ ٱلذُّلِّ ۖ وَكَبِّرْهُ تَكْبِيرًا ﴿١١١﴾

(10) Surah al-Mu'minun (23: 115-118)

أَفَحَسِبْتُمْ أَنَّمَا خَلَقْنَـٰكُمْ عَبَثًا وَأَنَّكُمْ إِلَيْنَا لَا تُرْجَعُونَ ﴿١١٥﴾ فَتَعَـٰلَى ٱللَّهُ ٱلْمَلِكُ ٱلْحَقُّ ۖ لَا إِلَـٰهَ إِلَّا هُوَ رَبُّ ٱلْعَرْشِ ٱلْكَرِيمِ ﴿١١٦﴾ وَمَن يَدْعُ مَعَ ٱللَّهِ إِلَـٰهًا ءَاخَرَ لَا بُرْهَـٰنَ لَهُۥ بِهِۦ فَإِنَّمَا حِسَابُهُۥ عِندَ رَبِّهِۦٓ ۚ إِنَّهُۥ لَا يُفْلِحُ ٱلْكَـٰفِرُونَ ﴿١١٧﴾ وَقُل رَّبِّ ٱغْفِرْ وَٱرْحَمْ وَأَنتَ خَيْرُ ٱلرَّٰحِمِينَ ﴿١١٨﴾

(11) Surah al-Saffat (37: 1-11)

بِسْمِ ٱللَّهِ ٱلرَّحْمَٰنِ ٱلرَّحِيمِ

وَٱلصَّٰفَّٰتِ صَفًّا ۝١ فَٱلزَّٰجِرَٰتِ زَجْرًا ۝٢ فَٱلتَّٰلِيَٰتِ
ذِكْرًا ۝٣ إِنَّ إِلَٰهَكُمْ لَوَٰحِدٌ ۝٤ رَّبُّ ٱلسَّمَٰوَٰتِ
وَٱلْأَرْضِ وَمَا بَيْنَهُمَا وَرَبُّ ٱلْمَشَٰرِقِ ۝٥ إِنَّا زَيَّنَّا
ٱلسَّمَآءَ ٱلدُّنْيَا بِزِينَةٍ ٱلْكَوَاكِبِ ۝٦ وَحِفْظًا مِّن كُلِّ
شَيْطَٰنٍ مَّارِدٍ ۝٧ لَّا يَسَّمَّعُونَ إِلَى ٱلْمَلَإِ ٱلْأَعْلَىٰ
وَيُقْذَفُونَ مِن كُلِّ جَانِبٍ ۝٨ دُحُورًا وَلَهُمْ عَذَابٌ
وَاصِبٌ ۝٩ إِلَّا مَنْ خَطِفَ ٱلْخَطْفَةَ فَأَتْبَعَهُ شِهَابٌ
ثَاقِبٌ ۝١٠ فَٱسْتَفْتِهِمْ أَهُمْ أَشَدُّ خَلْقًا أَم مَّنْ خَلَقْنَا
إِنَّا خَلَقْنَٰهُم مِّن طِينٍ لَّازِبٍ ۝١١

(12) Surah al-Rahman (55: 33-40)

يَٰمَعْشَرَ ٱلْجِنِّ وَٱلْإِنسِ إِنِ ٱسْتَطَعْتُمْ أَن تَنفُذُوا۟ مِنْ أَقْطَارِ ٱلسَّمَٰوَٰتِ وَٱلْأَرْضِ فَٱنفُذُوا۟ لَا تَنفُذُونَ إِلَّا بِسُلْطَٰنٍ ﴿٣٣﴾ فَبِأَىِّ ءَالَآءِ رَبِّكُمَا تُكَذِّبَانِ ﴿٣٤﴾ يُرْسَلُ عَلَيْكُمَا شُوَاظٌ مِّن نَّارٍ وَنُحَاسٌ فَلَا تَنتَصِرَانِ ﴿٣٥﴾ فَبِأَىِّ ءَالَآءِ رَبِّكُمَا تُكَذِّبَانِ ﴿٣٦﴾ فَإِذَا ٱنشَقَّتِ ٱلسَّمَآءُ فَكَانَتْ وَرْدَةً كَٱلدِّهَانِ ﴿٣٧﴾ فَبِأَىِّ ءَالَآءِ رَبِّكُمَا تُكَذِّبَانِ ﴿٣٨﴾ فَيَوْمَئِذٍ لَّا يُسْـَٔلُ عَن ذَنۢبِهِۦٓ إِنسٌ وَلَا جَآنٌّ ﴿٣٩﴾ فَبِأَىِّ ءَالَآءِ رَبِّكُمَا تُكَذِّبَانِ ﴿٤٠﴾

(13) Surah al-Hashar (59: 21-24)

لَوْ أَنزَلْنَا هَٰذَا ٱلْقُرْءَانَ عَلَىٰ جَبَلٍ لَّرَأَيْتَهُۥ خَٰشِعًا مُّتَصَدِّعًا مِّنْ خَشْيَةِ ٱللَّهِ ۚ وَتِلْكَ ٱلْأَمْثَٰلُ نَضْرِبُهَا لِلنَّاسِ لَعَلَّهُمْ يَتَفَكَّرُونَ ﴿٢١﴾ هُوَ ٱللَّهُ ٱلَّذِى لَآ إِلَٰهَ إِلَّا هُوَ ۖ عَٰلِمُ ٱلْغَيْبِ وَٱلشَّهَٰدَةِ ۖ هُوَ ٱلرَّحْمَٰنُ ٱلرَّحِيمُ ﴿٢٢﴾ هُوَ ٱللَّهُ ٱلَّذِى لَآ إِلَٰهَ إِلَّا هُوَ ٱلْمَلِكُ ٱلْقُدُّوسُ ٱلسَّلَٰمُ ٱلْمُؤْمِنُ ٱلْمُهَيْمِنُ ٱلْعَزِيزُ ٱلْجَبَّارُ ٱلْمُتَكَبِّرُ ۚ سُبْحَٰنَ ٱللَّهِ عَمَّا يُشْرِكُونَ ﴿٢٣﴾ هُوَ ٱللَّهُ ٱلْخَٰلِقُ ٱلْبَارِئُ ٱلْمُصَوِّرُ ۖ لَهُ ٱلْأَسْمَآءُ ٱلْحُسْنَىٰ ۚ يُسَبِّحُ لَهُۥ مَا فِى ٱلسَّمَٰوَٰتِ وَٱلْأَرْضِ ۖ وَهُوَ ٱلْعَزِيزُ ٱلْحَكِيمُ ﴿٢٤﴾

(14) Surah al-Jinn (72: 1-4)

بِسْمِ اللَّهِ الرَّحْمَٰنِ الرَّحِيمِ

قُلْ أُوحِىَ إِلَىَّ أَنَّهُ ٱسْتَمَعَ نَفَرٌ مِّنَ ٱلْجِنِّ فَقَالُوٓا۟ إِنَّا سَمِعْنَا قُرْءَانًا عَجَبًا ۞ ١ ۞ يَهْدِىٓ إِلَى ٱلرُّشْدِ فَـَٔامَنَّا بِهِۦ ۖ وَلَن نُّشْرِكَ بِرَبِّنَآ أَحَدًا ۞ ٢ ۞ وَأَنَّهُۥ تَعَٰلَىٰ جَدُّ رَبِّنَا مَا ٱتَّخَذَ صَٰحِبَةً وَلَا وَلَدًا ۞ ٣ ۞ وَأَنَّهُۥ كَانَ يَقُولُ سَفِيهُنَا عَلَى ٱللَّهِ شَطَطًا ۞ ٤ ۞

(15) Surah al-Kafirun (109: 1-6)

بِسْمِ اللَّهِ الرَّحْمَٰنِ الرَّحِيمِ

قُلْ يَٰٓأَيُّهَا ٱلْكَٰفِرُونَ ۞ ١ ۞ لَآ أَعْبُدُ مَا تَعْبُدُونَ ۞ ٢ ۞ وَلَآ أَنتُمْ عَٰبِدُونَ مَآ أَعْبُدُ ۞ ٣ ۞ وَلَآ أَنَا۠ عَابِدٌ مَّا عَبَدتُّمْ ۞ ٤ ۞ وَلَآ أَنتُمْ عَٰبِدُونَ مَآ أَعْبُدُ ۞ ٥ ۞ لَكُمْ دِينُكُمْ وَلِىَ دِينِ ۞ ٦ ۞

(16) Surah al-Ikhlas (112: 1-4)

بِسْمِ ٱللَّهِ ٱلرَّحْمَٰنِ ٱلرَّحِيمِ

قُلْ هُوَ ٱللَّهُ أَحَدٌ ﴿١﴾ ٱللَّهُ ٱلصَّمَدُ ﴿٢﴾ لَمْ يَلِدْ وَلَمْ يُولَدْ ﴿٣﴾ وَلَمْ يَكُن لَّهُ كُفُوًا أَحَدٌۢ ﴿٤﴾

(17) Surah al-Falaq (113: 1-5)

بِسْمِ ٱللَّهِ ٱلرَّحْمَٰنِ ٱلرَّحِيمِ

قُلْ أَعُوذُ بِرَبِّ ٱلْفَلَقِ ﴿١﴾ مِن شَرِّ مَا خَلَقَ ﴿٢﴾ وَمِن شَرِّ غَاسِقٍ إِذَا وَقَبَ ﴿٣﴾ وَمِن شَرِّ ٱلنَّفَّٰثَٰتِ فِى ٱلْعُقَدِ ﴿٤﴾ وَمِن شَرِّ حَاسِدٍ إِذَا حَسَدَ ﴿٥﴾

(18) Surah al-Nas (114: 1-6)

سْمِ ٱللَّهِ ٱلرَّحْمَٰنِ ٱلرَّحِيمِ

قُلْ أَعُوذُ بِرَبِّ ٱلنَّاسِ ۝١ مَلِكِ ٱلنَّاسِ ۝٢ إِلَٰهِ ٱلنَّاسِ ۝٣ مِن شَرِّ ٱلْوَسْوَاسِ ٱلْخَنَّاسِ ۝٤ ٱلَّذِى يُوَسْوِسُ فِى صُدُورِ ٱلنَّاسِ ۝٥ مِنَ ٱلْجِنَّةِ وَٱلنَّاسِ ۝٦

MANZIL COMPLETE (Transliteration)

(1) Surah al-Fatihah (1: 1-7)

1:1 Bi-smi-llāhi -r-raḥmāni -r-raḥīm(i)
1:2 Al-ḥamdu -li-llāhi rabbi -l-ʿālamīn(a)
1:3 Ar-raḥmāni -r-raḥīm(i)
1:4 Māliki yawmi -d-dīn(i)
1:5 'Iyyāka naʿbudu wa-'iyyāka nastaʿīn(u)
1:6 Ihdinā -ṣ-ṣirāṭa -l-mustaqīm(a)
1:7 Ṣirāṭa -l-laḏīna 'anʿamta ʿalayhim ġayri-l-maġḍūbi
ʿalayhim wa-lā -ḍ-ḍāllīn(a)

(2) Surah al-Baqarah (2: 1-5)

Bismillaahir Rahmaanir Raheem.

2-1. Alif-Laaam-Meeem
2-2. Zaalikal Kitaabu laa raiba feeh; udal lilmuttaqeen
2-3. Allazeena yu'minoona bilghaibi wa yuqeemoonas salaata
wa mimmaa razaqnaahum yunfiqoon
2-4. Wallazeena yu'minoona bimaa unzila ilaika wa maaa
unzila min qablika wa bil Aakhirati hum yooqinoon
2-5. Ulaaa'ika 'alaa hudam mir rabbihim wa ulaaa'ika humul
muflihoon.

(3) Surah al-Baqarah (2: 163)

2-163.Wa ilaahukum illaahunw waahid, laaa ilaaha illaa Huwar Rahmaanur Raheem.

(4) Surah al-Baqarah (2: 255-257)

2- 255. Allahu laaa ilaaha illa Huwal Haiyul Qaiyoom; laa taakhuzuhoo sinatunw wa laa nawm;
lahoo maa fissamaawaati wa maa fil ard; man zal lazee yashfa'u indahooo illaa bi-iznih;
ya'lamu maa baina aydeehim wa maa khalfahum wa laa yuheetoona bishai'im min 'ilmihee illaa bimaa shaaa';
wasi'a Kursiyyuhus samaawaati wal arda wa laa ya'ooduho hifzuhumaa; wa Huwal Aliyyul 'Azeem.
2- 256. Laaa ikraaha fid deeni qat tabiyanar rushdu minal ghayy; famai yakfur bit Taaghooti wa yu'mim billaahi faqadis tamsaka bil'urwatil wusqaa lan fisaama lahaa; wallaahu Samee'un 'Aleem
2- 257. Allaahu waliyyul lazeena aamanoo yukhrijuhum minaz zulumaati ilan noori
wallazeena kafarooo awliyaaa'uhumut Taaghootu yukhrijoonahum minan noori ilaz KwaZulu; ulaaa'ika Ashaabun Naari hum feehaa khaalidoon.

(5) Surah al-Baqarah (2: 284-286)

2-284. Lillaahi maa fissamaawaati wa maa fil ard;
wa in tubdoo maa feee anfusikum aw tukhfoohu yuhaasibkum
bihil laa;
fayaghfiru li mai yashaaa'u wa yu'azzibu mai yashaaa
u;wallaahu 'alaa kulli shai in qadeer.
2-285. Aamanar-Rasoolu bimaaa unzila ilaihi mir-Rabbihee
walmu'minoon;
kullun aamana billaahi wa Malaaa'ikathihee wa Kutubhihee wa
Rusulih
laa nufarriqu baina ahadim-mir-Rusulihee
wa qaaloo sami'naa wa ata'naa ghufraanaka Rabbanaa wa
ilaikal-maseer.
2-286. Laa yukalliful-laahu nafsan illaa wus'ahaa; lahaa maa
kasabat wa 'alaihaa maktasabat;
Rabbanaa la tu'aakhiznaa in naseenaaa aw akhtaanaa;
Rabbanaa wa laa tahmil-'alainaaa isran kamaa hamaltahoo
'alal-lazeena min qablinaa;
Rabbanaa wa laa tuhammilnaa maa laa taaqata lanaa bih
wa'fu 'annaa waghfir lanaa warhamnaa;
Anta mawlaanaa fansurnaa 'alal qawmil kaafireen.

(6) Surah Aali Imran (3: 18)

3-18. Shahidal laahu annahoo laa ilaaha illaa Huwa
walmalaaa'ikatu wa ulul 'ilmi qaaa'imam bilqist;
laaa ilaaha illaa Huwal 'Azeezul Hakeem.

(7) Surah Aali Imran (3: 26-27)

3-26. Qulil laahumma Maalikal Mulki tu'til mulka man
tashaaa'u
wa tanzi'ulmulka mimman tashhaaa'u wa tu'izzu man
tashaaa'u
wa tuzillu man tashaaa'u biyadikal khairu innaka 'alaa kulli
shai'in Qadeer.
3-27. Toolijul laila fin nahaari wa toolijun nahaara fil laili
wa tukhrijul haiya minalmaiyiti wa tukhrijulo
maiyita minal haiyi wa tarzuqu man tashaaa'u bighari hisab.

(8) Surah al-A'raf (7: 54-56)

7-54. Inna Rabbakkumul laahul lazee khalaqas sammaawaati
wal arda
fee sittati ayyaamin summmas tawaa 'alal 'arshi
yughshil lailan nahaara yatlu buhoo haseesanw washshamsa
walqamara wannujooma musakhkharaatim bi amrih;
alaa lahul khalqu wal-amr; tabaarakal laahu Rabbul
'aalameen.
7-55. Ud'oo Rabbakum tadarru'anw wa khufyah; innahoo laa
yuhibbul mu'tadeen.
7-56. Wa laa tufsidoo fil ardi ba'da islaahihaa wad'oohu
khawfanw wa tama'aa;
inna rahmatal laahi qareebum minal muhsineen.

(9) Surah al-Isra' (17: 110-111)

*17-110. Qulid'ul laaha awid'ur Rahmaana ayyam maa tad'oo
falahul asmaaa'ul Husnaa;
wa laa tajhar bi Salaatika wa laa tukhaafit bihaa wabtaghi
baina zaalika sabeela.
17-111. Wa qulil hamdu lillaahil lazee lam yattakhiz
waladanw wa lam yakul lahoo shareekun fil mulki wa lam
yakul lahoo
waliyyum minaz zulli wa kabbirhu takbeeraa.*

(10) Surah al-Mu'minun (23: 115-118)

*23-115. Afahsibtum annamaa khalaqnaakum 'abasanw wa
annakum ilainaa laa turja'oon
23-116. Fata'aalal laahul Malikul Haqq; laaa ilaaha illaa Huwa
Rabbul 'Arshil Kareem.
23-117. Wa mai yad'u ma'allaahi ilaahan aakhara laa burhaana
lahoo bihee
fa innnamaa hisaabuhoo 'inda Rabbih; innahoo laa yuflihul
kaafiroon.
23-118. Wa qur Rabbigh fir warham wa Anta khairur raahimeen.*

(11) Surah al-Saffat (37: 1-11)

37-1. Wassaaaffaati saffaa
37-2. Fazzaajiraati zajraa
37-3. Fattaaliyaati Zikra
37-4. Inna Illaahakum la Waahid
37-5. Rabbus samaawaati wal ardi wa maa bainahumaa wa Rabbul mashaariq
37-6. Innaa zaiyannas samaaa 'ad dunyaa bizeenatinil kawaakib
37-7. Wa hifzam min kulli Shaitaanim maarid
37-8. Laa yassamma 'oona ilal mala il a'alaa wa yuqzafoona min kulli jaanib
37-9. Duhooranw wa lahum 'azaabunw waasib
37-10. Illaa man khatifal khatfata fa atba'ahoo shihaabun saaqib
37-11. Fastaftihim ahum ashaddu khalqan am man khalaqnaa; innaa khalaqnaahum min teenil laazib.

(12) Surah al-Rahman (55: 33-40)

55-33. Yaa ma'sharal jinni wal insi inis tata'tum an tanfuzoo min aqtaaris samaawaati wal ardi fanfuzoo; laa tanfuzoona illaa bisultaan.
55-34. Fabi ayyi aalaaa'i Rabbikumaa tukazzibaan.
55-35. Yursalu 'alaikumaa shuwaazum min naarifiw-wa nuhaasun falaa tantasiraan
55-36 Fabi ayyi aalaaa'i Rabbikumaa tukazzibaan.
55-37 Fa-izan shaqqatis samaaa'u fakaanat wardatan kaddihaan
55-38 Fabi ayyi aalaaa'i Rabbikumaa tukazzibaan.
55-39 Fa-yawma'izil laa yus'alu 'an zambiheee insunw wa laa jaann
55-40 Fabi ayyi aalaaa'i Rabbikumaa tukazzibaan.

(13) Surah al-Hashar (59: 21-24)

59-21. Law anzalnaa haazal quraana 'alaa jabilil lara aytahoo khaashi'am muta saddi
'am min khashiyatil laah; wa tilkal amsaalu nadribuhaa linnaasi la'allahum yatafakkaroon.
59-22. Huwal-laahul-lazee laaa Ilaaha illaa Huwa 'Aalimul Ghaibi wash-shahaada; Huwar Rahmaanur-Raheem.
59-23. Huwal-laahul-lazee laaa Ilaaha illaa Huwal-Malikul Quddoosus-Salaamul Muminul Muhaiminul-'aAzeezul Jabbaarul-Mutakabbir;
Subhaanal laahi 'Ammaa yushrikoon.
59-24. Huwal Laahul Khaaliqul Baari 'ul Musawwir; lahul Asmaaa'ul Husnaa;
yusabbihu lahoo maa fis samaawaati wal ardi wa Huwal 'Azeezul Hakeem.

(14) Surah al-Jinn (72: 1-4)

72-1. Qul oohiya ilaiya annna hustama'a nafarum minal jinnni faqaalooo innaa sami'naa quraanan 'ajabaa.
72-2 Yahdeee ilar rushdi fa aamannaa bihee wa lan nushrika bi rabbinaaa ahadaa.
72-3 Wa annahoo Ta'aalaa jaddu Rabbinaa mat takhaza saahibatanw wa la waladaa.
72-4 Wa annahoo kaana yaqoolu safeehunaa 'alal laahi shatataa.

(15) Surah al-Kafirun (109: 1-6)

Bismillaahir Rahmaanir Raheem.

109-1. Qul yaa-ai yuhal kaafiroon
109-2. Laa a'budu ma t'abudoon
109-3. Wa laa antum 'aabidoona maa a'bud
109-4. Wa laa ana 'abidum maa 'abattum
109-5. Wa laa antum 'aabidoona ma a'bud
109-6. Lakum deenukum wa liya deen.

(16) Surah al-Ikhlas (112: 1-4)

Bismillaahir Rahmaanir Raheem.

112-1. Qul huwal laahu ahad
112-2. Allah hus-samad
112-3. Lam yalid wa lam yoolad
112-4. Wa lam yakul-lahu kufuwan ahad.

(17) Surah al-Falaq (113: 1-5)

Bismillaahir Rahmaanir Raheem.

113-1. Qul a'uzoo bi rabbil-falaq
113-2. Min sharri ma khalaq
113-3. Wa min sharri ghasiqin iza waqab
113-4. Wa min sharrin-naffaa-saati fil 'uqad
113-5. Wa min shar ri haasidin iza hasad.

(18) Surah al-Nas (114: 1-6)

Bismillaahir Rahmaanir Raheem.

114-1. Qul a'uzu birabbin naas
114-2. Malikin naas
114-3. Ilaahin naas
114-4. Min sharril was waasil khannaas
114-5. Al lazee yuwas wisu fee sudoorin naas
114-6. Minal jinnati wan naas.

REFERENCES

Ahmad, Muhammad Hambal. 2001. Musnad al-Imam Ahmad bin Hambal. Shu'ay al-Arna'ut & 'Adil Murshid (Ed.). Al-Qahirah: Mu'assah al-Risalah.

Al-Bukhari, Muhammad. 2001. Al-Jami' al-Musnad al-Sahih al-Mukhtasar min Umur Rasulullah SAW wa Sunanihi wa Ayyamihi – Sahih al-Bukhari. Muhammad Zuhair Nasir Al-Nasir (Ed.). Jld. 1-9. Masurah: Dar Tuq al-Najat.

Al-Darimi, Abu Muhammad Abdullah. 2000. Sunan al-Darimi. Hussain Salim Asad Al-Darani (Ed.). Jld. 1-4. Al-Mamlakat al-'Arabiyyah al-Sa'udiyyah: Dar al-Mugni li al-Nasr wa al-Tawzi'.

Al-Khandahlawi, Muhammad Zakariyya. t.th. Manzil. Lahore: Muhammad 'Abd al-Rahim.

The Qur'an and the Hadith. Unit 9, Islamic Correspondence Course. The MSA of the U.S. & Canada. Kazi, Mazhar, U. (compiled) (1406 A.H. - 1986 A.D.). A glimpse into the glorious Qur'an. American Trust Publications. Mawdudi, Sayyid Abul A'la (1988). Towards understanding the Qur'an. English version of Tafhim al-Qur'an. The Islamic Foundation. - - Translated and edited by Zafar Ishaq Ansari. Vol. II. Surahs 4 - 6. Murad, Khurram (1992). Way to the Qur'an. The Islamic Foundation. Leicester, United Kingdom. Siddique, Abdul Hamid (1987). Selection from Hadith. Islamic Book Publishers. Safat, Kuwait.

Ali, Abdullah Yusuf (1938). The meaning of the Glorious Qur'an. Text Translation and Commentary. Publishers: Dar Al-Kitab Al- Masri and Dar Al-Kitab Allubnani. Mawdudi, Sayyid Abul A'la (1990). The Holy Qur'an: Translation and brief notes with text. Islamic Publications (Pvt.) Limited.

https://sunnah.com/

http://www.quran-wiki.com/

https://islamicstudies.info

جزاك اللهُ خيراً

Please include me in your prayers.

Printed in Great Britain
by Amazon

21969849R00099